M000236319

How to BUY&SELL COLLECTOR CARS

Car Tech®

Patrick Krook

CarTech®

CarTech®, Inc.
6118 Main Street
North Branch, MN 55056
Phone: 651-277-1200 or 800-551-4754
Fax: 651-277-1203
www.cartechbooks.com

© 2022 by Patrick Krook

All rights reserved. No part of this publication may be reproduced or utilized in any form or by any means, electronic or mechanical, including photocopying, recording, or by any information storage and retrieval system, without prior permission from the Publisher. All text, photographs, and artwork are the property of the Author unless otherwise noted or credited.

The information in this work is true and complete to the best of our knowledge. However, all information is presented without any guarantee on the part of the Author or Publisher, who also disclaim any liability incurred in connection with the use of the information and any implied warranties of merchantability or fitness for a particular purpose. Readers are responsible for taking suitable and appropriate safety measures when performing any of the operations or activities described in this work.

All trademarks, trade names, model names and numbers, and other product designations referred to herein are the property of their respective owners and are used solely for identification purposes. This work is a publication of CarTech, Inc., and has not been licensed, approved, sponsored, or endorsed by any other person or entity. The Publisher is not associated with any product, service, or vendor mentioned in this book, and does not endorse the products or services of any vendor mentioned in this book.

Edit by Wes Eisenschenk
Layout by Chris Fayers

ISBN 978-1-61325-546-9
Item No. CT668

Library of Congress Cataloging-in-Publication Data Available

Written, edited, and designed in the U.S.A.
Printed in China
10 9 8 7 6 5 4 3 2 1

CarTech books may be purchased at a discounted rate in bulk for resale, events, corporate gifts, or educational purposes. Special editions may also be created to specification. For details, contact Special Sales at 6118 Main St. North Branch, MN 55056 or by email at sales@cartechbooks.com.

DISTRIBUTION BY:

Europe
PGUK
63 Hatton Garden
London EC1N 8LE, England
Phone: 020 7061 1980 • Fax: 020 7242 3725
www.pguk.co.uk

Australia
Renniks Publications Ltd.
3/37-39 Green Street
Banksmeadow, NSW 2109, Australia
Phone: 2 9695 7055 • Fax: 2 9695 7355
www.renniks.com

Canada
Login Canada
300 Saulteaux Crescent
Winnipeg, MB, R3J 3T2 Canada
Phone: 800 665 1148 • Fax: 800 665 0103
www.lb.ca

TABLE OF CONTENTS

INTRODUCTION

I wrote this book because there simply isn't one out there like it. There are plenty of books about the technical minutia of specific collectible cars, but there is not one resource focused on the skill of understanding which of those details most impacts the long-term value of each of those vehicles. There also is not a guide providing strategies for navigating the collector car marketplace— be it the private party sector or the auction scene. Each of those sectors has advantages and significant drawbacks.

Anyone who has surfed the internet for a high-quality collector car that is accurately presented will say first and foremost that the market is not set up with the buyer's interests in mind. Until now, people learned the collector car market the old-fashioned way: in the school of hard knocks. It seems some journeyman collectors are eager to pay that experience forward. There are few things worse than working your entire life to afford a cool collector car only to end up with a lemon and free ankle-grabbing lessons. That all ends now.

My mission in writing this book is to help buyers develop a sense of situational awareness within each environment, teach them how to use each to their advantage, and most importantly, teach them how to avoid being taken advantage of.

As a side benefit, buyers will also learn how to avoid costly purchasing mistakes. Some mistakes are made when buying a car that is simply misrepresented by the seller. Other mistakes that are just as costly and harder to detect are committed when a person buys the wrong car for the intended purpose. Worse mistakes are when buyers pass on the right car because they are emphasizing the wrong factors in their decision-making process.

This book may dive into the weeds a bit from time to time, but the journey is well worth it. You will come away as a more intelligent buyer with a higher quality of car in your garage and as a smarter seller when it comes time to move on to the next one.

We are all passionate about the car hobby, and it is about time we had fun with the process of buying and selling them as well. It is time to turn the tables and make the marketplace as enjoyable as the rest of the car hobby. So, let's go!

1

THE ROAD TRIP OF DESIRE BEGINS WITH THE END IN MIND

If you are reading this book, car parts (or maybe even an entire car) have probably been on your Christmas list more than once. Everyone has a different story of how he or she ended up at this point of obsession with all things automotive. I am certain that you know where it began for you.

Maybe it was as a young teen, shuffling through the high school parking lot watching the pebbles scatter when *it* is caught out of the corner of the eye. In a sea of ragged-out station wagons (or minivans) there was the car of your dreams gleaming in the sunlight as if a halo were radiating around it.

Maybe an older brother's best friend let you ride shotgun during a full-speed quarter-mile run in an open-top roadster, having to duck under the dash just to catch your breath as the car catapulted forward. Perhaps it was something different, but you know

the moment when you were transfixed, captured by the raw power and mind-altering lines of that car. It was . . . beautiful.

From that point forward, we were all in hot pursuit and determined to have that car in our garage—or at the very least, a car that reminded us of that moment. Let's be clear, it is not just a garage. It is a personal museum that, after a hard day or a long week, can be returned to time and again.

Maybe it is pulling a 10-second quarter-mile run on a factory-appearing car to revisit that place. The pursuit is different for each of us, yet we are all the same car people.

Finding the Right Fit

So, what exactly is the best way to find the right classic or collector car? Is there even really one best way? Yes, there is a right

Here's the end goal when either buying or selling a collector car. The whole process should leave both parties feeling good about the situation and know that professionalism and honesty were used throughout the experience.

way to search, evaluate, and secure a specialty automobile, and there are plenty of wrong ways to do it too.

"So, what exactly is the best way to find the right classic or collector car?"

The "how-to" is consistent no matter what kind of car is being hunted. The criteria will vary. The key factor that informs a strategy for buying the right car has little to do with what the car is and everything to do with how the car is being used by the current owner.

The best fit for a round peg is a round hole. Color, material, and height all can match, but if the peg is square, it simply isn't going to be a good fit. That is the same when looking to buy a collector car to enjoy. That is the key: joy.

If the current owner has enjoyed it the same way that the buyer aims to, chances are good that the car is of the quality and condition that will bring the buyer joy, and that is the point of collecting cars, isn't it? We call this principle use.

I know that it sounds elementary and perhaps unnecessary. Who cares what the last guy did with the car? We all want the same thing: the best. Everyone wants a number-one-condition car, right? If every auction description and classic car dealer advertisement is to be believed, they are all "number one."

Dialing in the Right Fit

Imagine for a moment that the car that just crossed the block on television lived up to its billing. Let's go further and bid on and win the car. It's now on its way home.

The car rolls out of the enclosed trailer, and the transporter gets the body inspection portion of the bill of lading signed off. There is not a mark; it is truly flawless. He directs attention to the undercarriage. Every nut and bolt gleams like new. The floor pan seams and pinch welds are impeccable.

Every clip, paint dab, inspection mark, and paper label are in place—just as it was the day the car originally rolled off the assembly line. The entire car is the same. This would meet the most understood definition of a number-one-condition car.

There is only one problem: The buyer also imagined driving the car cross-country, retracing historic Route 66. All the value would be driven right out of the car within

the first 100 miles. So, instead of spending time on the open road, meditating to the hum of the motor, time is now spent nervously chasing dust off the fender tops, running "Police Line Do Not Cross" tape through half of the garage.

Is this how they wanted to spend their time? Is driving the collector car they've been chasing their entire life supposed to induce an anxiety attack? As nice as this car is, clearly it isn't *their* number one.

There are many definitions of a number-one car. The key to enjoying the collector car hobby isn't getting sucked into a gravity well of cookie-cutter definitions, checking the boxes off a contrived list of absolutes. The mission is to find your number one.

This task is no different than Goldilocks sampling porridge. Some cars will be too sweet. Some will leave you lukewarm when viewed in person. Some will be just right. The best way to find the perfect porridge is to set down the checklist of "must haves" and think more broadly.

Have the money to buy the right car. What you are buying is how you are going to spend your time. You've paid your dues investing years taking care of "have-tos." Decide how you want to spend your personal time.

There are several ways people spend their time with their collector cars: project cars, daily drivers, seasonal drivers, driven show cars, trailered show cars, private museum pieces, and public museum pieces. Let's look at each type.

Project Car

This is usually the kind of car young buyers end up with, hoping to fix it up one day. Rarely do people have the money to restore their first project car, but it gives them proximity to the car of their desires and the ability to imagine how they are going to build, restore, or customize it.

A project car can be a purchase mistake if the buyer is buying on a limited budget, buying simply to "flip" and make a quick buck, or settling for one because they cannot seem to find a car to show and drive right away.

For older buyers who have more money and more experience, project cars present the opportunity to finish that vision from their youth. People who are into project cars and sell them almost as soon as they are complete enjoy the creative of process of returning something to its former glory or giving the car a new glory greater than it had during its first life.

A project car guy or gal most likely loves spending hours upon hours researching technical details, chasing

This is a classic example of "I'll fix it up one day." This 1973 AMX was sitting in a detached garage for decades. Would you leave it in barn-find condition or restore it? (Photo Courtesy Wes Eisenschenk)

This 1973 Caprice Classic convertible has been in the same family since it was new. For most of its life, it was driven daily, seeing many a Midwest winter before being relegated to the garage. Checking cars like these for rust issues is key to identifying the right car for driving everyday now or purchasing as a future restoration project.

down parts, and getting to know all the subject matter experts. They also tend to take the headaches in stride, whether doing the hands-on work or working with a qualified restoration shop.

Buying a car like this is a commitment to solve a million mysteries as much as it is creating something new. This kind of car is a "number one" if you enjoy the process as much as (if not more than) the finished product.

Daily Driver

A collectible car as a daily driver is either a vintage automobile that is complete, running, and in too good of shape to be relegated to project car stature or is a late-model niche vehicle that has a loyal fan base or is of limited production. In both cases, expect to see wear and tear in all areas of the car synonymous with being used as primary transportation with no one area being perfect. It is safe to reliably conclude that most of the factory-installed wear items people care to preserve are missing or replaced over the course of regular maintenance.

A daily driver buyer isn't concerned with preserving the car's originality if it means limiting the amount of time spent in the driver's seat. As Carroll Shelby famously stated, "These cars are meant to be driven, so enjoy the hell out of all of it—not just the look of it when it is all clean."

Now, this isn't a rust-belt winter beater; it is a nice car that is still used for daily transportation. If the gas tank is being filled twice or more a month, this is a daily driver.

The engine bay of a daily driver is a great window into how collector cars were personalized when they were just used cars. It is also the reason the buyer will be spending hours upon hours researching details and chasing down parts.

The engine bay of this Corvette looks clean enough for a driver. But a closer look reveals most of the factory-original wear items are long gone.

Buying a current or former daily driver can be a purchase mistake if you are looking for a car that has been pampered and carefully preserved during its life to buy as an unrestored, original example for investment. Buyers can also get taken in by a lower selling price of a driver when shopping for a show car, hoping to bring a daily driver up to a driven show car standard.

It is common to overpay for a daily driver compared to a project car and still end up spending the same in restoration costs. If the goal is to collect for fun and profit, that move is a profit killer, which kills the fun in the end.

Seasonal Driver

Compared to the daily driver, the seasonal driver cherishes his car like it's a slice of warm cherry pie ala mode—not all-you-can-eat ribs every Wednesday night. Taking the car out during the peak driving season and in fair weather only usually keeps the miles down and the normal wear to a minimum.

A 1963 Chevrolet Corvette split window isn't the first thing that comes to mind when thinking about a daily driver, but that is just what this is. The buyer of this car flew into Chicago in December and drove it all the way back to Utah through snowstorms. Drive the hell out of it, indeed.

A Word on Rust

It stands to reason that both daily driver and project cars will likely have rust issues, whether it is apparent or hidden. How much rust a car has is one of the key factors in determining whether a car is a good daily driver or a straight-up project car.

The rougher a daily driver becomes in overall condition, including how much rust it has, the more likely it slides from being the favorite ride into a place of limbo: a future potential project car. If it begins to have visible rust, the more likely it is that the car will be dumped, parked, or torn down.

Here is the undercarriage of the same 1973 Caprice Classic convertible. It is clear that the car has seen more than a few winters. The fact is, many daily drivers, even cars found in the South, bear some surface rust or grime on the frame and suspension parts. It is not show-quality material, but if the top side is clean and shiny, it can still serve as a good daily driver.

There is a big difference between surface rust (simply a scale of oxidation on the bare metal parts of the car and is usually found on the frame and suspension of the undercarriage) and structural rot. Structural rot is rust-through damage to areas of the car that is not easily repaired or replaced on the vehicle.

If the car looks good from 10 feet away yet has rust-through on sections of the frame, cowl, or body mounting tabs, that could lead to very costly repairs or a vehicle that cannot be salvaged. Enough of this kind of rust can take a car from being a daily driver past project car all the way to a parts car.

Also, consider rust from a safety perspective. If a car is being driven with undetected structural issues, it can cause an accident or fail to keep passengers safe in a crash. If the car doesn't have a solid foundation, all the hard work and money sunk into parts can also quickly turn into deep orange, metallic dust

This is the rocker panel of the same 1973 Caprice Classic convertible. Unlike the quarter panel, the rust through here is much more concerning. Rocker panels are a structural part of the body, even for body-on-frame cars like this one. The rocker panels carry part of the structural load, which is critical for convertibles such as this. Before buying this example, check to see if these rocker panels are reproduced or successfully fabricated. Evaluating structural integrity is about safety, not just good looks.

This bubbling around the rear wheel well looks bad. It likely means the quarter panel has to be replaced. That isn't as bad as it sounds. Many collector cars, even trailered show cars, have had quarter panels replaced as well as other exterior body panels. For a restored car, it is less about how much of the sheet metal is original and more about the quality of workmanship.

These cars are owned by those with impeccable habits. They usually spend more time primping and prepping the car than driving it. Historically, it also is commonly accompanied by a small flipbook memorializing every service event. Today, there are apps that track the same information.

No doubt the seasonal driver has tested each and uses the most effective one. Still, the car may see longer road trips, such as a Hot Rod Power Tour or a poker run with a local club. If it is going to be in a show, it will most likely be driven there. There is an increased chance of seeing road wear or getting caught in the rain. Hopefully, the seasonal driver details the car (undercarriage included) should he or she ever get caught in the weather.

The drawbacks to buying a vintage seasonal driver are really a matter of personal taste. The same personality type with the self-discipline and finicky nature also prefers restrained color pallets. Ever wonder why most every decent, unrestored, original-paint automobile is either some shade of green or brown? One of the possible pitfalls of chasing after one of these well-cared-for examples is finding a car that appears to be well cared for and highly original yet is neither.

Even the most detail-oriented buyer can get swept up in the emotion of finding a seasonal driver, but this one seems to have it all: eye-popping color combination, all the high-performance go-fast goodies, and at least some of the earmarks of a car that has been used for leisure most of its life. It is a purchase mistake not to scrutinize this kind of car.

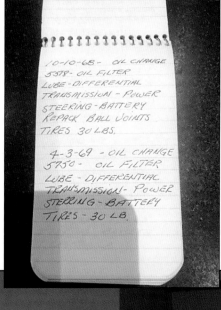

The odometer reads 12,323 miles, and most of them were clocked for the first 10 summers of its life. Short summers and good off-season storage habits made this 442 the investment quality example it is today.

No matter what kind of collector car is being purchased, the last owner's habits are being bought. The best way to know how the car was taken care of is to have its records. That 1967 442 was pampered.

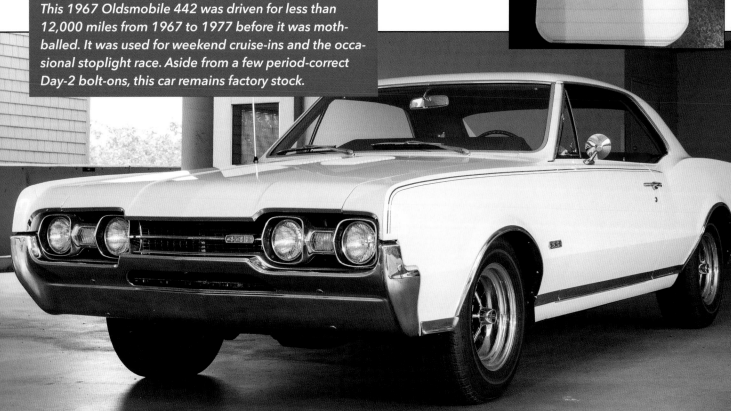

This 1967 Oldsmobile 442 was driven for less than 12,000 miles from 1967 to 1977 before it was mothballed. It was used for weekend cruise-ins and the occasional stoplight race. Aside from a few period-correct Day-2 bolt-ons, this car remains factory stock.

It takes real restraint to keep the miles down on a total performance machine like this 1996 Dodge Viper GTS. The 9,653 miles over 24 years averages to just over 400 miles a year. That is why this example still looks nearly new.

Restorers and speculators have become very adept at making a bone-tired drag race car appear to be a low-mileage original. The difference between a 12,000-mile summer driver and a 12,000-mile former drag racer is stark. One has traveled 500 miles a year for 24 years. The other has 48,000 quarter-mile passes under its belt.

Driven Show Car

This is a "cars and coffee car." A show driver probably isn't the first owner of the car, but he or she purchased the car totally restored or bought it as a pampered late model and is carefully keeping it preserved while driving on rare occasions.

If it is a late-model collectible (a 1996 Viper GTS, Buick GNX, C4-or-newer Corvette, etc.), this owner will want to keep the odometer reading below 10,000 miles or even 5,000 miles to maintain that distinction between a show car and a driver. While not a garage queen, this car only goes between 100 and 1,000 miles a year on the high side.

If the weather forecast shows even a 5-percent chance of rain, this car stays indoors and under a cover. More time is spent looking at the car, but it still gets driven enough to keep the seals supple and the fuel fresh. It is likely that this breed of automobile is trailered to all but the most local of events.

Often, driven show cars look attractive to a broad cross-section of buyers. The daily driver and seasonal driver may find this car too nice (and too expensive) to justify buying it just to drive the heck out of it. While some of the best driven show cars may have been restored to concours standards, there is a danger of buying a car that looks new and factory correct but requires extensive mechanical refurbishment to make it roadworthy. When talking to the owner, be sure to ask them how many miles they put on the car within the last year. Also, ask what their seasonal storage and maintenance routines are.

Most importantly, find out what work they have done to the car during their ownership and request the receipts to back it up. Lastly, always ask what they would do to the car if they were keeping it. This line of inquiry may give insight into any deferred maintenance or chronic problems that are waiting to vacuum that wallet clean.

Trailered Show Car

When most people think of a number-one car, this is what they think of. This is typically a car that was restored with concours showing in mind. These cars typically are only started and driven on and off an enclosed trailer. The most fanatical devotees to the concours lifestyle (and it *is* a lifestyle) even put "booties" or covers on the tires so that the treads do not pick up dust.

Some categories of concours showing do not require the owners to start or operate the vehicle, so they don't even have any fluids in them. The best way to avoid coolant and oil leaks is to not have any to begin with.

The problem with trailered show cars comes into play when it comes to driving them. A trailered show car may score 999 out of 1,000 points for Concours Gold and still require an extensive shakedown and mechanical tuning or even costly repairs to be roadworthy. So, when looking for a very impressive driven show car and considering if buying an older trailer queen is a good play, just make sure everything works before paying.

Cars like these are rarely, if ever, seen by the public. A rare jewel, waiting to be discovered, comes from private collections like this.

When buying any collector car of investment quality, know that the car is real, not just taking the owner's word for it. Having a car concours judged or independently verified by a third-party subject-matter expert can bolster its originality and authenticity.

Now, if the objective is to buy a trailered show car to continue showing it, it would be wise to have an expert well versed in the judging standards of the show to survey the car. He or she can make note of anything that will need to be updated, changed, or improved to compete at the highest level.

True number-one cars have a very short half-life. Between the ever-changing progression of judging standards and the natural decline that age puts on a car's finishes, there may only be a couple of show seasons before a car is retired from competition or requires a complete rework to remain competitive. That said, I have seen one or two cars that were restored to a high standard, carefully stored, and impeccably maintained to such a degree that the vehicle remains concours competitive 25 years after its initial restoration. This is the exception to the rule, but it is one worth noting.

Private Museum Piece

This *is* the garage queen. Whether it is 1, 2, or 225 cars, private museum pieces are purchased and often never see the light of day until they come out to be sold. Private museum owners are just that: private. These cars

Some of the most unique and historically significant collectible cars can be found in public museums.

are rarely, if ever, shown in public. One or two may pop up at an invitation-only car show, but not at the annual spring fling or cars and coffee event.

Most owners of this ilk don't like the spectacle or judgment of their cars being picked over or picked on at a concours event. If you know about these cars or the collection, it's because you know the owner. This type of collection, and this type of collector, is mostly about one thing: the self-gratification of automotive sanctuary.

The best public museums have a maintenance routine to keep their vehicles in good mechanical condition. Here is a 1971 Plymouth 'Cuda Hemi 4-speed valued at $1.5 million getting ready for its exercise run.

There isn't anything inherently wrong with this. A collector has a vision to assemble the best of his or her beloved makes and models. Often, the collection is used as a backdrop for entertaining friends and family and enjoying the solitude of comfy leather chairs and the beautiful view of chrome and steel. If car fanatics were to design their ideal church, the floors would be filled with private museum pieces and the walls decked with neon.

When buying a private museum piece, the owner's personal preferences as well as his or her selection skill are purchased. If the buyer has a learned eye and the discipline to buy only "the best," then a buyer is likely to end up with an excellent car that hasn't popped up at every auction for the past five years. This is a rare jewel waiting to be discovered, and that is the advantage of buying from a private museum collector.

If you are buying to add to your own private museum collection, the downside of buying a private museum piece is really limited to repeating the same purchase mistake that the current owner made. You could possibly be picking up the tab for any maintenance deferred during the previous ownership.

There is nothing worse for an automobile than for it to sit. Seals dry out, tires rot, freeze plugs leak, fuel gets stale;

it is car abuse. If an owner says something like, "It has the same mileage on it as it did when I bought it 10 years ago," just know that a hefty bill may be coming to recondition the car to roadworthy status. That isn't a museum piece; that is a car that has been kept in cold storage.

The other possible risk to buying a car out of a long-term private collection is one of authenticity. Often, questions such as, "Does it have the original motor?" or "What was done during restoration?" are met with confident, affirmative answers. This is because the owner is confident about what he was told by the previous owner, not because he verified it himself. Always ask the follow-up question: "How do you know?" If the answer is "Because the previous owner told me so," then decide if the car is worth verifying or passing on it to find a more well-documented example.

Use the "Ask an Expert" Lifeline

Engaging an independent third party with expertise in verifying VINs is always a great idea, one that is easier to invest in if the car already possesses some provenance to begin with. The same is true for a fully restored car.

Most private museum pieces have been rotisserie restored. The value of that restoration is both in how correct it is and the quality of the workmanship. That is best illustrated by how extensively documented the restoration effort is. The bottom line is to buy something that can be proven as genuine and genuinely well cared for. If the seller cannot prove it, then don't pay for it. We will cover both authentication and provenance more extensively in later chapters.

Public Museum Piece

Most automobiles that are on public display at a museum are on loan from private collectors. Occasionally, a private owner will open his or her entire collection to the public. In either case, these cars remain on static display for a long time and are there to do one thing well: tell a story. Often, these represent the rarest and most remarkable examples of their kind or hold some historical significance. Both of those factors certainly boost the collectability of a car.

Even for the private collector, buying a public museum piece can make sense. They are often considered to be the best of the breed, and it depends upon the prestige of the museum collection in which it was a part. The reputation of the collection, and sometimes even the collector, can boost the value of a given car.

On the flip side, a car that has been kept in a public setting can also fall into disrepair. Worse, inattentive staff can leave the cars exposed to the ravages of the public pawing the car. I've seen a kid licking an ice cream cone while peering into the cockpit of a multi-million-dollar 427 Cobra. Good thing the kid didn't lean on the aluminum fender!

This all comes down to the museum's maintenance routines. How long has this car been on display? What are the maintenance protocols? How often are the cars exercised? Knowing the answers to these basic questions can make the difference between buying the crown jewel of your own collection and purchasing a very pretty project car.

As was said earlier, there is little worse for an automobile than for it to sit. They are machines that are happiest when they are run regularly. Most cars that sit on static display in even the most well-run museums never start or move from the time they are lent out for display to the time they leave. So, what may seem to be a prestigious purchase that will impress a buyer's peers can quickly turn into a maintenance nightmare compounded by a pile of unanticipated repair bills. That famous public museum car is now an infamous public embarrassment. Take time, look past the fancy display, and note the evidence of deferred maintenance or neglect often inherent in these kinds of cars.

When people think of a number-one-condition car, tl what they think of: a trailered concours show car. This usually the only time a public museum piece will be s outside the museum: when it has been invited to a ju car show. This 1970 Plymouth Superbird Hemi 4-spee being judged at the Muscle Car and Corvette Nation (MCACN) in 2014. It was awarded Concours Gold.

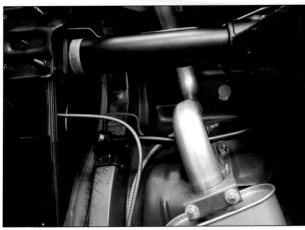

Keeping a concours car in number-one condition is a never-ending battle. Even a small matter like the wat stained paper label on the axle or a mild oxidation o the exhaust clamp are enough to hold a car back fro competing at the highest level.

The odds are good that you are not one of the p stepping up to the plate to purchase a multi-millior lar Cobra or a million-dollar Hemi 'Cuda. Few peopl Few museum cars are in this category anyway.

Even for an entry-level collector who is shoppi the $10,000 to $35,000 range, the information h still useful. There are hundreds of public museums a the country and the world that showcase cars ir price range. Every car needs the same care and is su to the consequences of neglect when sitting in stati play, regardless of its estimated value. It is more im ant to detect and address any deficiencies in this m range because the repairs are often proportionately expensive than the same work needed on a higher-dollar car. More of the anticipated return is gobbled up in remedial repairs.

Now, after reading through these commonly used categories for collector cars, you either said to yourself, "That sounds like me" or more likely, "There is no way in blue blazes I would do *that* with a car." Either way, congratulations! You are clear on the objective to buying a special-interest automobile.

More importantly, you have come to the realization that the best person to buy such an automobile from has been using it in the same way that you plan to. There are also high costs to be paid if buying a car that was used for a purpose other than one you intend. Sometimes, if buying a car out of advantage, the changes you wish to make can be priced in, but don't count on the seller to subsidize your personal vision for the car. Everyone puts money into a car once he or she buys it. That is part of making it your own.

Finding a Car

It is time to talk about some overall strategies and mistakes in finding a car. Each one of these kinds of cars from the project car to the trailered show car requires a different strategy to source, evaluate, negotiate, and secure the vehicle. It isn't as simple as showing up at a local auction event or scrolling through the automobile marketplace ads online. A lot of time can be wasted looking for cars in the wrong places.

Patience Pays

Buyers looking for an impulse purchase to use for fun without concern for the financial ramifications can step right up to the next auction event. There, a 20- to 30-percent premium is paid for convenience, which is not unlike buying milk at the gas station but with TV cameras and better production values than the local Kum & Go.

If a show-quality driver is wanted, go to car shows and see what catches your eye. Scouring thousands and thousands of internet classifieds, online auction sites, and social media marketplaces may also be a possibility, but it may mean weeding through many cars for a long time before finding the right one. Then, go see it in person, or at least have it inspected before completing the purchase.

If you are buying primarily for investment purposes and building an investment-quality collection, then it pays to be patient and selective. The right car may never be publicly advertised. Those that do show up at auction

or in the classified pages may very well be worthwhile but require expert scrutiny. Even a subject matter expert can be fooled while performing an auction-site inspection, especially without knowing the history of a car. Either way, it becomes a matter of who you know. In the long run, being patient pays large dividends.

Savvy sellers also use patience to their advantage, paying attention to what is currently hot in the market and bringing those cars to public shows. One such frenzy that took many by surprise was the barn-find craze. Most of these cars were essentially project cars that fell into disrepair and were relegated to the corner of the garage with an attitude of "I'll restore it one day." Cars like these used to be an affordable source for a potentially high-end project car.

When cars like these began to be featured in TV shows, such as *American Pickers*, and books, such as Ryan Brutt's *Amazing Barn Finds and Roadside Relics*, a few barn-find cars went for big dollars at public sales. Then, they started to show up in featured displays, including the Muscle Car and Corvette Nationals' (MCACN) Barn Find sections and the for-sale row at various shows. The patient seller saw the market trend, and "I'll restore it one

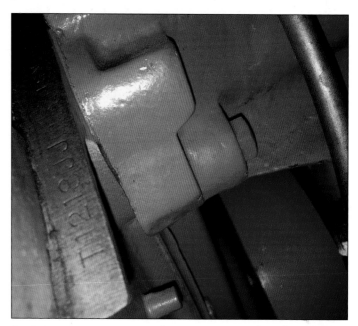

Restamps are more prevalent on some makes than others. Chevrolets see the highest occurrence of unoriginal motors that are numbers matching, due in part to national points judging organizations that mandate that a car has a VIN-stamped motor to be eligible for a Concours Gold. Highly desirable big-block Chevrolets are also the easiest to fake without original factory documentation. Other marques acknowledge the hard life of the typical muscle car by permitting a documented factory warranty replacement engine with no points deduction.

Watching a shiny car being pushed off the auction block with the bid stalled at a low number is a great temptation. If that is the first time seeing the car, do yourself and your pocketbook a favor and sit on your hands.

day" became "I'll cash in now." Even if a car doesn't find a buyer at the show, it can leave a positive impression when displayed properly. Afterward, the car has an addition to its pedigree.

"Featured at MCACN's Barn Find Display" becomes an accolade setting it apart. It isn't just a barn find; it is *that* barn-find car. So, just as buyers are looking to get the most value for their dollar and stay just ahead of emerging trends, the sellers are also positioning their cars to earn the most money by capitalizing on them. This is the dance.

You Can't Take Back Time

When it comes to committing a purchase mistake, money is hard to recuperate; time is impossible to replace. I've spoken to one avid concours collector who only purchases cars that are documented and still retain their original engines. He personally flies in to see each prospective purchase before completing a deal.

This buyer reports as many as 15 percent of the cars that claim to have their original motors end up having restamped engine blocks. Yes, this kind of hands-on due diligence can help avoid buying the wrong car, but it cannot buy back the time spent away from business and family just to be let down by an owner who, either out of ignorance or malicious intent, materially misrepresents a vehicle.

Buying a Car or 15 Minutes of Fame?

If you haven't experienced it, then you have heard similar horror stories from friends. That person who headed to an auction not really planning on buying anything but attended just to have a good time. Bright lights, television cameras, and the right number of adult beverages combined with being near all that gleaming chrome and shiny paint can result in an impulse purchase.

The resulting headache isn't just from the hangover the next day; it lives on when the actual car arrives at his garage. He goes over the car to confirm he's made a good purchase, and well, now he sees the car for the first time n full daylight and sober. Then, he realizes that the hangover from that auction weekend is going to last for quite a while, and the headache has just begun.

How much did it cost for the weekend of spontaneous fun? Do the math. Take your annual income, divide it by an average of 2,080 working hours in a year. How much time was spent chasing cars that didn't pan out? How much time was spent straightening out a rolling mess instead of enjoying a car? That is in addition to the unanticipated hard costs of making a car stand up to its original billing.

Then, there are the uncountable opportunity costs. What else could have been done with that time? Enjoying time with family? Perhaps actually relaxing for a change? Those hours wringing hands and clenching teeth are gone.

Buying another crisis to manage is the number-one reason people are blown out of this hobby. It just isn't fun to spend time and hard-earned money to fight yet another fire. We do that every day in our business and personal lives. Car collecting is supposed to be both a reward and refuge.

As pretty as an OEM factory-correct restored undercarriage is, it is far from ideal for a car intended for driving. All of the dollars spent on the OEM detail and pristine condition of the chassis will be lost before the first tank of gas is burned through.

Ordering the "Number One" with a Side of Anxiety

Even if the ideal car is a daily driver or a drivable project car, wasting irretrievable time and money on travel or auction fees doesn't have to be limited to drastic examples such as these. Even if a buyer gets the best car money can buy and it's real and right, it can still end up being a purchase mistake.

Suppose for a moment that no matter where the car was purchased, it arrives and is exactly as it was expected to be. The paint-by-number rules were followed for buying a collector car, chasing the "Number One" myth. However, now the car is here, and it is a good car but isn't a good fit for how the buyer wants to use it. The car becomes another source of anxiety, not relaxation. There is such a thing as being too nice.

Once it is decided which purpose is the best fit for a buyer's lifestyle and collecting goals, that determines where money should be spent. There is no sense in buying a 30-year-old car with delivery miles on it, only to drive the car 5,000 miles a year. It is possible to pay a 25- to 50-percent premium over the price guide value for a car with an original motor and broadcast sheet. However, is that the best use of money if the goal is to drive the Hot Rod Power Tour every summer?

For less money, a non-numbers-matching car or a small-motored base model that can be customized to tour with can be purchased. Otherwise, for those with deeper pockets, purchase a Full Custom build with state-of-the-art pro-touring technology and creature comforts for the same money as a pedigreed OEM car and have more fun.

This is just one example. It doesn't matter what is being collected or what make or model a buyer desires, these principles hold true. No, I am not suggesting that there are one-size-fits-all metrics that can be used as a checklist to buy any and every collector car. These are strategic fundamental principles, not technical solution tactics.

Follow Your Heart but Keep Your Head

The first principle is to only buy what you love. It sounds counterintuitive, doesn't it? Aren't I supposed to be logically detached to make the best possible purchase decision? The answer is yes—to a point. It isn't a commodity or an apartment complex that is being bought here. You are going to be emotionally involved in the purchase, so you may as well use that to your advantage rather than suppress it. Suppressing the impulse to act on an automobile gives that impulse all the power to come out in ways that cannot be controlled. So, keep that desire in mind.

Buy what you love because you probably know more about that kind of car than others you are only mildly interested in. Developing a deep well of knowledge regarding a make and model of car also comes in handy when doing due diligence on a promising candidate for a collection.

When spotting an exciting car, use that excitement to dig deeper into the car before emotions take over. The natural inclination is to look for things that confirm the idea of purchasing the car. The multi-billion-dollar social media industry is based on this single human trait: playing to confirmation bias. So, if you really, really like something, go in the opposite direction; lean hard on it and really scrutinize it.

The harder you look for reasons *not* to buy, the more the discovery will reveal that this is the right car or show exactly why it's not. This results in the immediate joy of finding "the one" and a long-lasting satisfaction of a prudent purchase decision. These reasons should be squared against the plan for using the car (principle use) and the factors that impact the value and collectability of the make and model. Those factors are not one size fits all.

As a seller, it is natural to lose interest in a car before it is sold. That is likely the reason it is being sold. However, remember that failing to address the small details, which are those things buyers look for to select the right car or formulate their offer, will cost money or making the sale at all.

Prepare the car as if it is being taken to a show, taken on a long road trip, or both. Take away as many of the problems the car has as possible. Plainly disclose anything you are unable or unwilling to address and price that problem into the offering number. That way, you cannot be leveraged into bargaining against yourself due to an unknown or undisclosed problem with the car. You may even receive more interest and higher offers for being candid. Many people have a problem being truthful (or at least objective) when selling a car. Being both earns a seller credibility and a confident buyer. Those two things are priceless.

On average, people keep their collector cars for about three to five years. Some are long term or lifetime collectors. Each type of collector wants to make sure they are getting the best deal they possibly can. Unchecked, this can lead to passing on cars that are an excellent fit for the buyer's intended use and selection criteria but are a few

thousand dollars more than the last one that was passed on. The last one wasn't a winner because the buyer knew they wouldn't be happy with it once they got it home.

Buying a collector car is about finding the car that represents the best overall value, not the cheapest price. This is not an actuarial exercise. Is there an investment aspect to these cars? Of course. That is why they are considered collector's items.

"Is there an investment aspect to these cars? Of course."

Choosing the right car means it will be enjoyed no matter how the market performs over the next several years. The right car brings a smile every time it is seen no matter how soft the market is. The right car is something the buyer will want to keep even if someone offers stupid money for it. The right car leaves fond memories no matter what it sells for whenever it is time to send it to the next caretaker.

It isn't all about the money. Remember, this is about building an experience. We build businesses and make stock market investments to make money to provide for our families. We invest money in collector cars to create and share memories with our families.

Bring Money Habits from Business but Don't Make It Another Business

"I'd walk a mile for a Camel." Remember that old cigarette advertisement? That was the Madison Avenue adman's way to say that what you know is true about anything you love. It means having a tolerance for the headaches that naturally come along with anything that you genuinely care about. The same goes for classic cars.

With cars come car problems, no matter how carefully the selection process is at the time of purchase. It's a good thing that love brings with it a heaping helping of patience. Conversely, buying something just because the price was right is like hitting your thumb with a hammer because you had a coupon for the hammer.

This is what happens when the automobile collecting hobby is turned strictly into another business. First, it is no longer a relaxing pastime; it is another job. Second, if the car was bought with no emotional connection and strictly for investment, it is more likely that a purchase error will be committed. I've seen it on the auction block; a good-looking car stalls well short of the auction's estimated range. A guy sticks his hand up in the air like econd grader who is eager to offer the teacher the right nswer. They take his bid, lift the reserve, and hammer he lot closed. "Yes! I got that one cheap," he whispers o his friend.

As it turns out, the car was a color change and converted from an automatic to a 4-speed manual shift. The catalog description didn't disclose any of that, and because he didn't know these cars very well, well, he didn't know what to look for. The heartburn sets in. It only gets worse when he gets the car home and realizes that the entire fuel system needs to be replaced and carburetors rebuilt for the car just to run properly. Fed up, he hits the eject button and dumps the car on Craigslist for pennies on the dollar just to get it out of his sight, compounding the loss.

Simply looking for "opportunity buys" and not caring about or knowing that car's details, the chances go up exponentially that one will be bought with hidden headaches. There is also a lower tolerance for costly repairs and higher anxiety if the market for them goes down. In other words, if you own something you don't like, you will almost always find a way to lose money on it. Discount hammer, meet thumb.

Bucket List

Make another Christmas list of the cars that you know and love and want to own. Learn what traits make each of those cars interesting in general and personally desirable. Decide how to spend your time with them and prioritize the selection criteria to identify the best of that kind in the marketplace.

Once it has been determined how you will best enjoy the car, that dictates both where you are likely to find it and what makes that a perfect fit for you. That is what we cover next: the factors that make cars collectible. Understanding this shaves weeks or even months off your search time and saves you thousands, both upfront and in the long run.

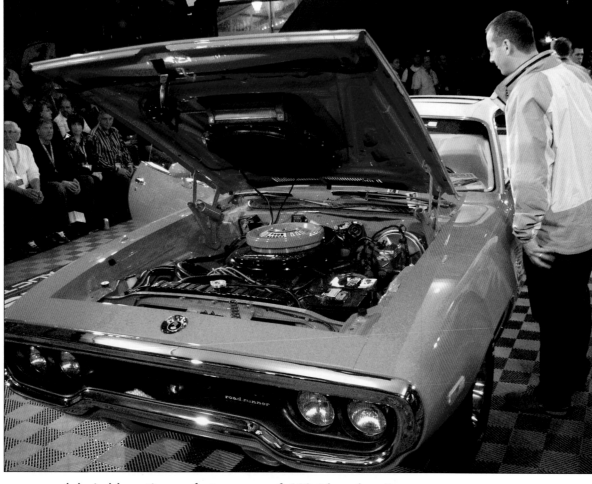

Once committed to purchasing a collector car, plan and avoid hunting a bargain for a bargain's sake. Trying to quickly assess the market on the block for a make and model you are unfamiliar with is an invitation to calamity. Getting caught up in the drama will result in paying much more than planned. This 1972 Plymouth Road Runner GTX (offered at no reserve in 2011) was optioned with some rare and desirable options: a factory sunroof, 440 4-barrel engine, and a 4-speed manual transmission. When the dust settled, the car fetched $121,000. The 10-year auction average for a 1972 GTX is $40,878. Let's hope the winner of this car was dead set on checking off the last box of his bucket list, no matter the cost.

2 THE BUYER'S KEYS THAT MAKE A CAR COLLECTIBLE

Imagine discovering a car on your Christmas list that no one knows about. The history of the car is known back to new. The engine and transmission are original right down to the plug wires. The paint and body are original and flawless. The interior looks like the day the original selling dealer first pulled the plastic off the seats. Every page of factory documentation, including the original dealer sales contract and window sticker, are present and accounted for. Turn the key, and it instantly rumbles to life, driving out like a dream. What is it worth?

Desirability Is Key: The "Gotta Have It" Factor

By the way, the car is a 1967 Chevrolet Corvette roadster 427/435-hp L88 in Tuxedo Black with a red leather interior and Red Stinger hood stripe. What is it worth now? Hold on, I meant a brown-over-tan 1963

Is that dream car worth more to you than it is the next guy?

Chevrolet Corvair endowed with an 80-hp flat six. What is it worth *now*?! The answers respectively are the following: invaluable and unvaluable.

I hold no judgment against the person who has his or her heart set on a Corvair instead of a Corvette, but I included it in this illustration for a reason. The collectability or collective value of a given make and model is not driven by personal tastes. Collector value is driven by how many other people in the market at large also have that car on their Christmas lists. When in acquisition mode, it may benefit a buyer to have an odd taste in cars. It may also cost the buyer on the back end when it is time to sell.

The "It" Car

The best time to buy a car is before it is a *thing*. That is to say, before it bubbles up into public consciousness as something that everyone wants. There are a couple of examples of this that can be readily appreciated.

Muscle cars of the 1960s and 1970s have long established themselves as having broad and sustained market desirability. They are well positioned to continue to hold their value after the generation that bought them new has passed on. Within that genre, a few makes and models have risen to the top of the "Gotta Have It" rankings throughout the years. It is possible to look at the 1970–1971 Plymouth Barracuda Hemi convertible and follow

If you have ever imagined owning a 1969½ lift-off-hood Road Runner, this is it. High-impact "Gotta have it" color? Check. A genuine, factory A12 code car? Check. Factory-original drivetrain? Check. Extensive owner history backed by paper records? Check. Excellent condition, nearly showroom new? Check. All five keys of collectability are in this one car.

General Motors was looking to make this the American Beetle. By 1963, it was on its way with more than 900,000 units sold. It was even the subject of a book published in 1965 that is now considered an American classic. But by 1969, only 6,000 Corvairs were made. The book by Ralph Nader was Unsafe at Any Speed, *which transformed Corvair from icon to infamous in just a few years even though the design issues cited had already been re-engineered by the time the book was published. Despite falling victim to an early form of media manipulation that seems commonplace today, the Corvair has a modest yet persistent following. There is a Corvair Museum, a Corvair Preservation Foundation, and a club called the Corvair Society of America. With 4,000 members and 120 local chapters worldwide and more than 1.7 million made during nine years of production, plenty survive today for those fans to choose from.*

Here is the fire-breathing heartbeat of Nader's night-mare, making a mere 80 hp. There are no official fatality figures for Corvair. I am willing to bet more people have died driving a Corvette than a Corvair at any speed. Between the maligned reputation, uninspiring engine output, and ample supply, the "Gotta Have It" factor is low.

Any car with current or future collector potential embodies one thing: a big, hairy, audacious proposition that is well executed. In the muscle car era, that meant performance and personalization was for everyone, not just the caviar crowd. It was whatever captured the collective imagination and left a permanent impression on their minds. Now, it is how much technology can be packed into a passenger compartment motivated by 100 percent of torque available at zero RPM. Those will be in the collections of the future.

hem from being invisible in the marketplace to being at he very top of the muscle car pantheon.

The reason is simple: when the 'Cuda convertibles vere new, convertibles, in general, were on the very end of decline of public demand. A convertible model was a ignificant added cost to the options list and the Hemi engine itself tacked on nearly 30 percent of the base price o the vehicle, which was much pricier than air condiioning. Air conditioning, as the technology became nore compact, reliable, and affordable, led to the death of the convertible.

The 426 Hemi engine, by the way, was none of those hings. By 1972, virtually all major manufacturers had eliminated or drastically reduced their convertible modls within their lineups, and they were mainly relegated o their premium divisions. Convertibles tended to weigh nore and were also more flexible than their closed-coupe counterparts. For those who wanted to competitively race one, it required a cage with a roll bar to pass safety inspecion—and the Hemi engine, that was for drag racing, right?

So, there it is. An overpriced convertible in the budget Plymouth line was not very prestigious and had an expensive Hemi in it that was at a competitive handicap rom the outset. Did I mention it could not have air conlitioning with it? It is no wonder that so few were ever ordered. It was an audacious and impractical idea, which s why most people during that time bought a small-block Mustang with air conditioning instead.

It doesn't have to be a multi-million-dollar Hemi-powered muscle car to be a highly desirable collector car. Cars like these (1971 Hemi 'Cuda convertible), only a few years after they sold new, could be had for as little as $1,500, and sellers had a hard time getting it. (Photo Courtesy Ola Nilsson)

By 1973, a Hemi-powered car could not even be given away. The gas crisis led many to shelve their high-performance engines and go hunting for a junkyard slant-6 to get as much gas mileage as possible out of their former pony car, just to get through to the next ration day.

By 1973, the big-block Corvette was only making 275 hp.

This version of the Chevy 454 was a shell of its former self. In a market dominated by horsepower numbers, the LS4 was meh. Boost the compression and you have a fire-breather. To the shade-tree mechanic, it was a big-block bargain.

By 1973, in addition to being down on power, the Corvette no longer wore the chrome blade bumper up front. Add to that the Dark Yellow Metallic, and it does not make the top of most collector's lists. This one, though, sold for good money because it is one of the most desirable unrestored examples of its kind.

The keys and strategies laid out in this book will help you identify and capitalize on the next up-and-coming 1971 Hemi 'Cuda. It may also prevent you from paying too much for a future classic whose future never arrives.

Leading the surge in SUV popularity is the first-generation Bronco. Built between 1966 and 1977, the boxy 4x4 was very attainable up until the mid-2010s. An explosion in popularity occurred with the announcement of the return of the Bronco nameplate and the introduction of the Coyote engine that has found a home in the modified versions of these trucks. (Photo Courtesy Wes Eisenschenk)

Catch a Wave

Ideally, the point of this is to catch the wave of collectability before it gets to millionaires fighting with billionaires for the best of the best and the rarest of the rare. The next wave may look nothing like the past.

So, how can a buyer tell what the next Hemi 'Cuda convertible will be when, right now, it looks like the Pontiac Aztec? It sounds absurd, right? Well, go find the issue of *Motor Trend* magazine that covered the first look at the 1971 Plymouth 'Cuda. It was a scathing rebuke of all of the key styling attributes that make the car so sought after today: the sawtooth front grille, the fender gills; all of it was thoroughly panned. *Motor Trend*'s conclusion was that there's always next year.

Now, this does not mean that the Pontiac Aztec is suddenly beautiful, but it is going up in desirability by a young audience looking for something different and affordable in a land dominated by overpriced look-alike crossovers. Aztec's design looks more at home in today's landscape that it did when it was introduced. Its "go-go-gadget" features and accessories make it endearing to those who are willing to buck the conventional wisdom of these ugly ducklings.

Like another quirky, underpowered people mover, the VW bus, the Aztec is building a cult following. People are starting to care about the car. Before saying, "Just wait a minute, you are crazy. There is no way an Aztec will ever be collectible," just remember that people routinely now pay $100,000 plus for a custom restored VW bus.

4x4 in Today's Marketplace

If that is a bridge too far to cross, let's look briefly at the current mega-dollar 4x4 craze. How much is a 1972 Chevy K5 Blazer worth? A few years ago, a solid driver could be picked up for $5,000 to $10,000. Recently, a custom-restored K5 sold in an online auction for $305,000!

That is a long way from being budget back-40 beaters. Usually, that is how it starts: a model is plentiful and affordable, and people create a community around sourcing parts, maintaining, rebuilding, and eventually restoring or customizing a given model.

In the social media age, creating and growing those communities has never been easier. To know what the next emerging *it* is, check out the growth rate of the online communities dedicated to it. The same goes for the "king of the hill" marques: the Porches, the Mustangs, and the Corvettes of the world. The more enthusiasm (and fewer problems) that later models have, the more likely that they will have an enduring collectible value in the future.

Authenticity

The Pontiac Aztec argument may seem ridiculous, but only time will tell if it is or not. Desirability is subjective and changes over time as tastes change. Sometimes it changes as generations of buyers mature into the marketplace. Sometimes it changes as our relationship to the vehicles themselves change.

The black 1967 with a red stinger hood and side pipes certainly looks the part of the iconic L71 427 Corvette. With the hood open, the engine bay reveals a small-block 327. It is perfect for driving, but big-dollar collectors need to have the big-block. This tempts many unscrupulous speculators to take a tastefully personalized car like this one and finish the conversion, passing it off as the real thing.

The proliferation of so many clones and restamped 427 tri-powered 1967 Corvette Roadsters have diminished the value of genuine, unrestored examples such as this. This car has lived in the same town in which it was sold new. Locally, it is well known and accepted as authentic. The car also does not have any documentation, no Monroney Label, and the tank sticker is unreadable. Getting top dollar in a national market leery of fakes would prove to be difficult, even with the endorsement of a professional inspector.

"Desirability is subjective and changes over time as tastes change."

If collective demand over time outstrips supply on a sustained basis, then the collector value can skyrocket. Regardless of whether you find Porsche GT RSs or Pontiac Aztec GTs desirable, the primary driver of collectible value is also informed by other factors: authenticity, originality, pedigree, and condition. We will tackle authenticity first because if the car is not the genuine article, then it is not much else.

The real thing is not a substitute, a clone, or a "tribute." Canadian inventor Elijah McCoy devised a machine for lubricating engines that was so successful that it spawned many copies, and all were inferior to the original. He patented the design in 1872, coining that often-repeated phrase along with it. As cars have moved from mere appliances to collectible kinetic art objects, the industry of taking lower born vehicles and altering them to pass as the genuine article has grown with it.

The temptation to alter or augment a real car to boost its desirability, or simply create one out of thin air for either greed or glory, has proven to be too great to resist for many throughout the automotive collecting industry. This can be anything from adding factory-correct options to a car that was not originally equipped with them or changing the color of the body and/or interior from something drab to a more exciting color combination and then attempting to pass it off as factory equipped.

Most common in certain sectors is swapping out non-numbers-matching engine and transmission assemblies with ones that appear to be original, restamped with the vehicle's original VIN. Other schemes include duplicating factory-original paperwork (protect-o-plates, warranty cards, build cards, broadcast sheets, and Monroney labels, which are more commonly known as the window stickers) all in an attempt to pass the car off as original.

The age-old contest between lock maker and lock pick rages on here as well. If it boosts the salability or perceived value of the car, people have attempted it. Some of these bad actors are darn good at it too.

The standards for judging Corvettes have contributed to the problem. A date code–correct, VIN-stamped engine is required in the car to win Concours Gold. So many people with real cars wanted that "first place" trophy but had a car with a service replacement block that a cottage industry of locating date code–correct engine blocks and faking the factory VIN markings grew up around the hobby like a poison ivy vine wrapping itself around an oak tree.

The problem has become so invasive that the major auction houses post large disclaimers on the footer of video screens stating: "Unless otherwise expressly stated,

Counterfeit Cars

More 427/435-hp Chevrolet Corvette roadsters are on the road today than General Motors ever built in 1967. The proliferation of so many counterfeit cars has led to the diminished value of some genuine yet hard-to-document originals. That is the most glaring illustration of this problem in today's collecting climate.

assume each vehicle does not have its original, numbers-matching drivetrain."

As judging standards for authenticating these vehicles has changed, the fraudsters have evolved as well. It is to the point now that if a 427/435-hp 1967 was judged before 2008 and had an original tank sticker, the authenticity of the car is in question. There are now people who counterfeit Monroney labels and tank stickers (complete with artificial aging) that are nearly undetectable unless forensically scrutinized. It is a real fun-suck in a high-stakes hobby that is supposed to be, well . . . fun! So, what is one to do?

Plenty of people who have been burned by this type of shenanigans abandon the hobby. I suggest not giving

General Motors did not publish a serial-number database for these or other high-performance models from the 1960s, making it ripe for profiteers to create 427/435-hp clones from a plentiful supply of their small-block brothers. Deciphering whether the VIN on this block is factory or counterfeit has become a science unto itself. Passing off a restamped motor could mean the difference between Top-Flight and Second-Flight judging accolades at NCRS events. It could also mean the difference between owning an affordable small-block driver and a big-dollar payday at the expense of an unwitting collector.

This is one worth digging deeper into to make sure it's worth the asking price. This 1967 Corvette is a two-owner L89 427/435-hp roadster. Only 16 of them were made. Since an L89 is an L71 427, but with aluminum heads, they too are prone to being cloned. This one, owned by only two people who were friends since the car was new, has sound provenance but is short on factory documentation. It is well worth the effort to have an acknowledged expert authenticate the VIN stamps, casting codes, and date codes on the drivetrain assembly. Even though this car is the real McCoy, the collector value would nearly double if it also had factory documentation.

he greedy jerks the satisfaction. Resist the natural urge of confirmation bias, find reasons to buy the car you are excited about, and develop a healthy skepticism.

The more you like a car, the deeper you should dig into the guts of it, finding reasons not to buy it. If there is nothing objectionable, then you have successfully used your mind to guard your heart, and you have full permission to love it. It is time to marshal your resources and do some detective work.

Private Eye

Determining authenticity is a look at the car in its totality and seeing if all the other factors hang together. The simplest example is seeing a five-digit odometer that reads 6,000 miles and then looking at the brake pedal pad and ignition lock to see if the wear indicates the car indeed has 6,000 miles or possibly 106,000 miles.

Double-check by looking at all the belts, hoses, clamps, and plug wires. A 6,000-mile car will usually still have its original consumables under the hood. Next, check expired registrations and copies of previous titles for reported mileage. Is it ever more than 6,000 miles? If not, and condition, originality, and documentation all point to the same thing, then the odometer reading is most likely authentic. But authenticating an entire car goes much deeper than that.

Jump through all these hoops to make sure of one thing: the car finally sitting in your driveway after spending so much time parked in your mind is indeed real. People value the truth, and it feels good to have a longtime dream come true.

If the car isn't authentic, that dream just becomes a deceptive illusion and a lie that you must tell yourself and everyone who asks, "Is it real?" If the lie is repeated often enough, the joy being pursued while chasing that car becomes a corrupted source of anxiety. Or worse, you fall into the trap of telling yourself that the fact that it isn't real doesn't matter. If you sell yourself on that idea,

Just like the yellow 1973 Corvette Stingray that was shown earlier, this 1972 Plymouth Duster is a prime example of originality. Even with more than 60,000 miles on the odometer, it still wears its original paint, original interior, and completely unrestored engine bay and undercarriage.

then you have far bigger problems than whether the car was factory issued.

If authenticity becomes a question of, "Can I make people believe this is real?" instead of "How can I prove without a doubt that this car is real?" then the seller bears the burden of wondering when their cleverness will finally run out and how it will come back to bite them. They are no longer pursuing happiness or enjoying the peace of free time with a well-earned reward. That is something you really do not want—not in your garage and not in your mind. Guard your heart and protect that joy that you set out to find in the first place. Make sure the car you are buying is authentic or at least that the purchase wasn't based on a lie.

Originality

The most desirable, well-documented, and intact cars in excellent condition are more valuable than the same car that has been fully restored, no matter how well it has been redone. The reason is simple: it is the genuine article. It is like fresh-squeezed orange juice rather than reconstituted. It is only original once.

The best way to determine if a car is the real McCoy is to see it in original, unrestored condition. The benchmark for originality is a completely unrestored vehicle that still contains all its original components and is in new or nearly new condition when compared to when the car first rolled onto a dealer showroom floor. The car speaks for itself.

Instantly Collectible

The earliest example of when people were buying cars new and simply "putting them away" on a large scale was 1978. Corvette owners were excited by the arrival of the 25th anniversary in 1978, and they ordered Silver Anniversary Edition and Corvette Indy Pace Car Replicas—even telling the dealership not to prepare the

The Saturn Sky Redline and its platform cousin the Pontiac Solstice GXP are affordable examples of cars people were excited about, purchased, and simply put away as an instant classic. Examples still in the wrapper are holding a value at or above their original window sticker.

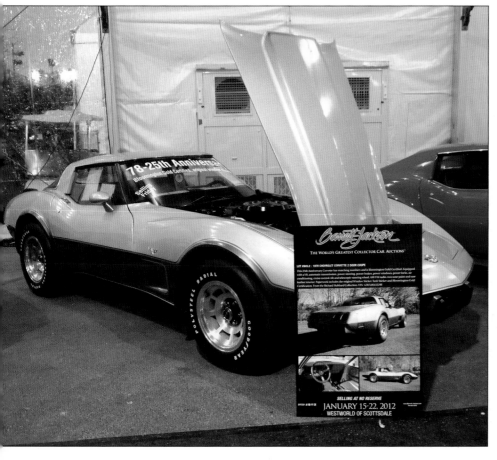

Here, awaiting its turn on the auction block, is a pristine example of the more affordable special-edition Corvette offered by Chevrolet in 1978: the 25th Silver Anniversary. This one is touting the distinction of being Bloomington Gold Certified and still possessing its original window sticker. Nearly half of total Corvette sales that year ended up being one of these not-so-limited editions. Many people paid double the original $12,164.89 sticker price when these were new. The result is a perpetually saturated market of 1978 Silver Anniversary and Indy Pace Car editions. Perhaps predictably, the famous "Barrett-Jackson effect" was no factor here, and the sale price of $19,800 was $1,500 less than NADA or CPI Black Book at the time of the sale.

vehicle for the showroom. The plastic covers were still on the seats and steering wheel, which is the epitome of "in the wrapper."

The Silver Anniversary Edition was essentially a paint option priced at $399, and it was a popular selection with 15,283 units built, which represented 33 percent of the total production. The special-edition Pace Car Replica, celebrating 25 years of Corvette, had a base price of $13,653.21 ($4,300 more than the base Corvette).

So, many people bought the Pace Car package as an investment, and 15 percent of the total production were Indy replicas. One can still be found at most any auction with plastic still in place. With both the Silver Anniversary and Pace Car editions being special but not limited editions, together they accounted for nearly half of total production that year.

That's not so good if you are looking for a high return on investment, but it is exceptionally good if you are looking to verify that what you are buying is exactly as it was when it was new. Heck, the Monroney label is still in the window. From about the 1990s forward, more people were buying cars new and simply putting them away on a regular basis. The standard of what is considered investment quality has also been raised with this trend. It is much harder to discern what is original and what is restored or altered the further you go back into automotive history.

Now, paying an enormous premium while caught up in a new car frenzy does not always spell doom for those screaming "Take my money!" This scenario played out again in 2005—this time with Ford and its much-touted Ford GT. The original manufacturer's suggested retail price (MSRP) was $149,995. Most people paid a healthy dealer markup from $10,000 to $50,000 more than sticker price. The original production plan was 4,500 cars. Between the 2005 and 2006 model years, a total of 4,038 cars were produced. Today, these cars are worth more than twice or three times their original MSRP.

Unlike many other modern performance vehicles, the market value of the Ford GT has not dipped below the original asking price. Its second-generation successor, priced at $450,000, entered production in the 2017 model year and is scheduled to continue through 2022 with 250 cars built annually. Most of those have sold on the secondary market for more than $1 million. That is an instant collectible.

Historic Restorations

Some prewar-era cars (1930–1940) are nearly impossible for the average enthusiast to benchmark as a surviving original because the restoration work itself is 50 years

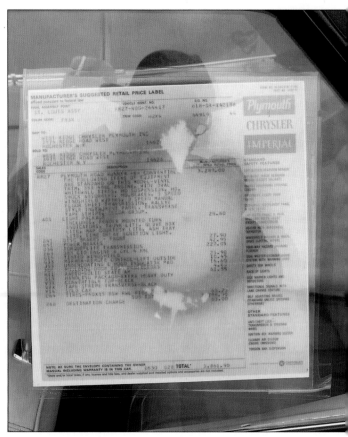

The Monroney label is named after Almer Stillwell Mike Monroney, a United States senator from Oklahoma. Senator Monroney sponsored the Automobile Information Disclosure Act of 1958.

old or more. How manufacturers documented major options (drivetrain combinations, colors, and trim levels) are less apparent.

By 1958, manufacturers were mandated to put a window sticker (Monroney label) on the window of each car outlining how the car was equipped and the added cost for each option.

It was not until the early 1960s that it became easier to tell what the factory-original color and trim options were without a window sticker, thanks to more data being included on body trim tags. Some manufacturers codified the engine into the VIN and included major options such as transmissions, rear-end ratios, and power options on their trim tags.

Federal Mandates

By 1968, every maker was federally mandated to stamp the VIN on the engine and transmission of the vehicle, in addition to the body and VIN plate. When looking at an original, understored, high-performance automobile, understand that it is an uphill battle. Cars that were purchased, kept in the shipping plastic, and

It is not only factory originality that is preserved on unrestored cars but it is also how they were used and what was popular during the time they were new. I wonder whatever happened to Appliance Industries; the company had a cool header logo.

promptly put into climate-controlled storage are an exception to the rule.

Planned Obsolescence

Most muscle car–era vehicles started out with a factory-planned lifespan (planned obsolescence) of three or four years at 8,000 to 10,000 miles a year. (The days of 100,000-mile warrantees were still a long way off.) Then, the Big Three manufacturers (Ford, General Motors, and Chrysler) wanted buyers to purchase another new one.

They did not count on us falling in love, either. Sadly, the muscle cars we love the most (the ones painted flashy colors with big-block motors and 4-speed transmissions) are also the ones that have lived the hardest lives. There is no telling what lurks beneath the lipstick-red paintwork that has been Zymoled within an inch of its life.

Even by the mid-1980s when the pony car wars returned (Camaro versus Mustang), most gearheads went right to work building up the motor and shaving weight. Power was up compared to the malaise era of the late

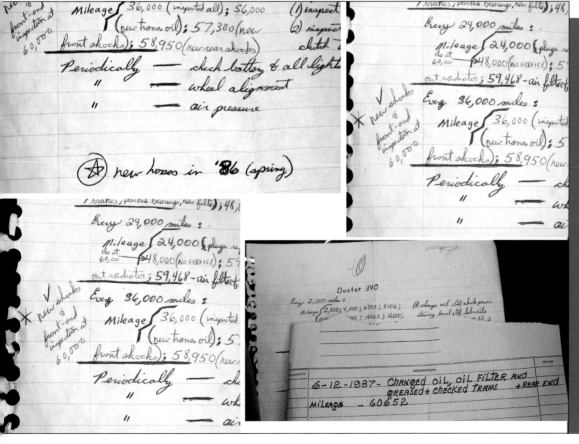

Sometimes, looking into the engine bay of a car will show what is original and what has been replaced as part of regular maintenance. In addition to the car itself bearing witness to the life it has led, an original car also tends to survive with its original owner records. This will give you a hint as to why the car has remained in such good condition over the years.

This is a 1971 Chevrolet Corvette LS6 454, recipient of both the NCRS Bowtie Award for Preservation Excellence and the Duntov Mark of Excellence Award. These two awards combined designate this LS6 as the benchmark of originality and correctness for an unrestored, factory-original Corvette. It also means that this car is turnkey and road ready, just as it was when it rolled off the showroom floor 50 years ago. This grade of authenticity is a force multiplier of collectable value.

1970s but just barely. Intakes, heads, throttle bodies, emissions systems, and factory power adders were commonly canned in favor of the hottest aftermarket performance parts. Even if the car was not modified, original parts were not high quality and were also replaced regularly during a car's normal service life.

News and Notes

A potential collector car may have had a dozen owners or more. Information gets lost, memories fade, and what the current owner was told by the previous seller becomes the new gospel truth. Even the most honest and objective owners can be simply misinformed. A fan of a make and model since it was new will likely have his or her own frame of reference to start from regarding how an original car should be presented. Instead of relying on the accuracy of how the car is represented by the owner, it is important to le the car speak for itself.

Most originality purists look on concours trailer queen the same way most compare a cloned car to a factory born performer. This breed of collector gives on condition in favor of preservation. Interestingly, those who chase the concours trophies often look to these surviving examples to benchmark their recreation of factory delivered condition. The collectors interested in these aspects of the hobby do not get to drive their cars that often, or at all.

Preservation

The preservationists and the concours collectors have something else in common: hours spent obsessing over the minute details, memorizing every detail and variation that the factory produced. Find a club discussion board or social media group and listen, learn, and build a knowledge base to add to your own experience.

Become familiar with the key common components that are prone to excessive wear or failure. More importantly, find out which parts are nearly impossible to replace. A car missing most of its irreplaceable parts will not hold its value as well as one that still retains them.

Moreover, far more than the difference may be spent in cash comparatively when attempting to source parts that are made of "unobtanium" sometime in the future. This is especially important to remember when collecting modern performance vehicles.

Manufacturers do not maintain a spare parts catalog going back decades. Currently, it may even be difficult to find common wear items for vehicles that are fewer than

Most ultra-low-mile muscle cars that have been restored along the way probably looked like this 3,000-mile 1970 Dodge Challenger T/A F Stock NHRA drag racer. The Gypsy was purchased new right off the showroom floor in Boise, Idaho, and was immediately prepared for drag racing. Those with nationally renowned drivers or titles were preserved or restored in as-raced trim. The rest were reconstructed back to stock street trim and sold as low-mile originals, even though those miles were likely driven a quarter mile at a time. This one earned three national records and remains unrestored in its own way in as-raced form still wearing the race livery originally painted in 1970.

This 1987 Buick Grand National GNX shows only 7,000 original one-owner miles. It is unaltered from the OEM factory specifications, even wearing its original belts, hoses, plug wires, and tires. The paint work is 100 percent original. The interior is 100 percent original. The word survivor *was intended to describe a car like this.*

10 years old. A new old stock (NOS) gas cap for a vintage restoration project may cost $800 not because it is made from gold bullion but because there are not any more to be found. It may pay to keep a personal stock of factory-original service parts for your car while they are still easy to source if the plan is to keep it long term.

"Low Mileage" Does Not Always Mean Original

Some people hunt for the lowest-mile car they can find as a definitive indicator of originality. It is more likely that the Plum Crazy Hemi Super Track Pack 'Cuda with 2,000 original miles on it has 8,000 passes at the drag strip than it is a carefully preserved car. Truth be told, many former drag stars had their odometers disconnected. That is why so many "low-mile" muscle cars have been restored because they really needed it.

A low-mile automatic big-block car with a non-original transmission or a low-mile 4-speed car with a replacement block might be a drag car. That is not the end of the world; it's just a fact of the life that these cars led.

If they have been completely restored, does it matter how hard the miles were? In a word, *yes*. Both a fully restored car with a ton of hard miles on it or one that has seen more than a few quarter-mile passes will not feel as solid and tight as one that was driven regularly under normal conditions.

Do the math. If a vintage car was normally driven 8,000 to 10,000 miles a year and was generally expected to last four years, then the average odometer reading for a car should range between 32,000 and 40,000 miles before falling out of regular use. Add another 20,000 to

30,000 miles for pleasure driving over the past 30 years, and the car has an average of 65,000 miles for a typical life. It is hard to tell what kind of things a car has seen just by looking at the mileage. So, check all the factors, documentation, condition, and originality of common wear items, which give odometer reading context. Let the car speak for itself.

Real Originality

There is no single shortcut indicator to tell if a car is 100-percent original. Since low mileage is not an automatic indicator of getting a highly original car, there is another option that has the added benefit of guilt-free driving. It is often described as a "survivor with one repaint." These are driver-quality cars that have likely been incrementally refurbished over the years. Frankly, they are often too nice to take all the way down to a nuts-and-bolts restoration.

A numbers-matching, well-documented driver represents a good value to the individual enthusiast. Preservationists do not want them because the original paint is gone and the concours crowd likes to look for "done" cars that may only need detail correction. Even the collectors looking for a winter project are likely to pass because they can find one in rougher shape for a cheaper price.

So, there it is, the high school dream car aging gracefully after all these years. It will likely have an intact owner history, receipts of repair work, and maintenance logs. It will also have likely never had its motor yanked or body stripped bare.

A well-kept car will also have a subtle patina. The expert who was recruited to help make a good purchase can tell what about this driver gives evidence to normal wear or abuse. Checking the numbers on the drivetrain, body, and glass are all part of gauging the depth of its originality.

The paperwork that goes with the car should check out against what can be seen. If the car shows the normal signs of aging and is otherwise intact, grab it. This is a car that can be driven and enjoyed today, and when it comes time to restore it, you are starting with a more original car than most. A highly intact car means few hard-to-find parts in the future and a more original car than most others when finished.

Pedigree

All of the contributing factors that make up a car's pedigree have limitations: internet history, pre-internet history, factory documentation, licensed factory database reports, owner records, restoration records, third-party

This is the undercarriage of a 1973 Chevrolet Caprice Classic convertible that has been sitting in the family garage for nearly 30 years.

inspections, and judging sheets. Taken together, they paint a pretty complete picture of what a car was born as, how it was used during its life, and what the quality of the car is today. The golf course car show crowd calls this provenance. In common "car guy" tongue, it is proof that this car is real, original, and right.

Restoration or Resurrection?

For a completely restored car, the car's past life is harder to ferret out. Expect a complete photo album documenting the car's restoration from beginning to end. Even if every floor pan and quarter panel has been replaced, it is better to know the worst than to suspect it.

If a freshly restored car is not accompanied by photographic evidence, a pile of receipts, and a logbook of parts replaced, move on to one that is. The undocumented job was likely rebuilt for a quick resale.

If careful concours-quality restoration using NOS parts was performed and the process was not meticulously documented, it will not receive credit for all the work when it comes time to sell. Without the documentation, no one will know the difference and will likely assume the worst. The entire car becomes a black box, leaving a buyer to wonder what this UFO looked like before they got it.

How Is the Car Used Most?

When buying a restored car, having the restoration documented is important for establishing its integrity and future valuation growth, but it is not the most important thing. How the car was enjoyed throughout its history is more important than how it looks in

"CONCOURSE QUALITY, HOBBYIST PRICE"

MartiAutoWorks

DELUXE REPORT

Official Licensed Product®

5012

Proud to display this symbol

Copyright Kevin Marti 2009

www.martiauto.com
12007 W. PEORIA AVENUE
EL MIRAGE, AZ 85335
(623) 935-2558
(623) 935-2579 Fax

Thank you for your interest in our services. We have determined the following information for your car from the Ford Database we have:

VEHICLE ORDER IMAGE

12345678901234567890123456789012345678901234567890123456789012345678901234567890

U BA 7 12B9472   UM3D L6C T 7   2   &11B067 BV

DOOR DATA PLATE INFORMATION

Serial Number

1970

Built at Metuchen

Mustang Sportsroof

302-4V Boss Engine

53,007th Ford vehicle scheduled for production at Metuchen

Built: January, 1970

Mustang Sportsroof

Grabber Orange Paint, Ford #3659-A

Black Rhino/Corinthian Vinyl Bucket Seats

4.30 Locking Axle Ratio

Four-Speed Close Ratio Manual Transmission

Boston Ordering District

ORDER TYPE LOCAL PROMOTION
DSO ITEM #: 9472
DEALER#: 11B067
JACK MADDEN FORD SALES IN
825 PROVIDENCE
NORWOOD MA 02062

Your vehicle was ordered with the following features:

Rear Deck Spoiler
Four-Speed Close Ratio Manual Transmission
Locking Differential
Optional Axle Ratio
F60X15 Belted Tires w/ Raised White Letters
Sport Slats
AM Radio

MANUFACTURED BY
FORD MOTOR COMPANY 153007

01/70 THIS VEHICLE CONFORMS
TO ALL APPLICABLE FEDERAL
MOTOR VEHICLE SAFETY STAN-
DARDS IN EFFECT ON DATE OF
MANUFACTURE SHOWN ABOVE.

VEHICLE IDENT. NO.	BODY	CC
	63A	U
TRIM	AXLE	TRNS	DSO
BA	W	6	11

NOT FOR TITLE OR REGISTRATION

MADE IN U.S.A.

IMPORTANT DATES:

ORDER RECEIVED:	12/30/69
CAR SERIALIZED:	01/20/70
BUCKED:	01/23/70
SCHEDULED FOR BUILD:	02/12/70
ACTUALLY BUILT:	01/23/70
RELEASED:	04/03/70
SOLD:	04/30/70

STATISTICS

Your car was one of:

2,752	With this Paint Code
2,042	With these Paint/Trim Codes
4,607	With these Engine/Transmission Codes
1,869	Ordered from this DSO
4,443	With Sport Slats

For the 1970 Mustang Sportsroof.

Your car was actually produced on January 23, 1970 -- twenty days ahead of schedule.

Kevin Marti

Kevin Marti

Facing page: Some vintage cars are easier to document than others. This is a Marti Report for a 1970 Ford Mustang Boss 302. It is much harder to clone a vintage Boss Mustang than it is a vintage big-block Corvette or Chevelle because of historical database reports like these. They are an invaluable resource to hobbyists seeking to fill in the blanks that missing factory paperwork creates.

photographs or even in person now. The first question to ask the current owner is: "How is the car used most?" This gets back to the idea of principle use. It is a good bet that if the answer matches your plans for the car, then you are probably going to be happy with the purchase.

Going back further, does the available documentation establish how the car was mainly used throughout its life? If it was a dragster, it will have piles of time slips and pictures of it at the strip back in the day. If it was a weekend cruiser, then it should have a maintenance logbook and perhaps pictures of the car at the local show with the kids posing next to it. If it was a regular driver, perhaps there are repair receipts chronicling service history as the miles piled up on the odometer.

Mundane Collector Cars with Pedigree

Ironically, it is the green and brown cars with the base engine and automatic column shift transmissions that seem to come with the most paperwork. It makes sense: organized and practical people also buy boring cars. But these violate the first key of desirability. We can all agree that it does not matter how original or how clean the owner history on the car is if it is not anything we want.

The truth of the matter is, the more desirable the car, the more important the documentation is. The risk that someone with designs of a fat profit resurrected a genuine big-block, 4-speed car from a former life as an outdoor chicken coop is more likely than a kindly grandmother wending her way to church every Sunday in her Yenko Camaro. Even more likely, that grandma's 230 I-6 3-speed Grecian Green base coupe was transformed into that icon of Camaro performance.

Factory Databases

Production databases are a handy tool for establishing that the VIN on the title and the dash are in fact that highly prized apex predator you are hunting down. However, these databases for each maker in this era vary wildly. Chrysler has historical information for cars that were produced in 1967 and older. Ford's North American production database is available through a third-party licenser from 1967 to 2017. General Motors does not have publicly available production data for Chevrolet products, but Pontiac and Buick factory records are available.

These records are often used in conjunction with fac-

tory documentation to corroborate one another. If the original documentation on hand matches what is in the factory database, then odds are good on having the real McCoy.

Factory Documentation

The same holds true for the factory documentation itself. Factory documentation is the current standard by which most collectors stake the authenticity of a car. Build sheets, window stickers, original sales contracts, warranty books, and advanced shipping notices are exciting to have along with the car. They are vital clues to how the car was originally ordered, delivered, and sold to the first owner.

Sadly, most original documents that can be presented with the car can also be counterfeited or altered to bolster a false claim. That said, if there is a copy of an original broadcast sheet and the details match the available factory database records, then you can have confidence that the document reflects how the car was originally equipped.

Beware: the more a car is potentially worth, it is more likely that unscrupulous people will attempt to produce fake paperwork to either boost the value of a genuine car that is missing original paperwork or use counterfeit paperwork to add a veneer of legitimacy to an equally counterfeit car.

Judging Sheets

Concours awards and judging sheets are useful to the extent that they are evidence that the car was inspected by a team of marque experts and compared to an excepted standard of excellence. The veracity of this information is tempered by how precise the judging system is. A 400-point judging system at one show is not going to describe the quality of the car as well as a 4,000-point judging system. Also, the age of the judging score also impacts how well it describes a car against a given standard.

Concours standards are in a constant state of evolution, hopefully one of consistent improvement. A National Corvette Restorers Society (NCRS) National Top Flight Award conferred in the 1990s is not equal to one awarded this year. Become familiar with the scoring system used by the governing body that pertains to the car you are considering to give those judging sheets context.

For instance, do points awarded for "numbers matching" mean that the VIN stamp on the engine pad is consistent with other factory exemplars—merely that the

Facing page: This is a broadcast sheet for a 1970 Chrysler product. They were used by line workers to assemble the vehicle with the correct equipment as ordered by the dealership. Every manufacturer had its own version. The best way to tell how your car is supposed to be equipped is to look at the sheet that autoworkers used to build it in the first place. Notice the marks running diagonally across the page. Those are seat-spring marks. Most of the broadcast sheets recovered by owners of vintage Chrysler products were discovered sandwiched between the springs and foam on the underside of the back seat.

engine casting code is consistent with the year, make, and model of the car without regard to what is stamped on the ID pad or if it looks correct or obviously not? The details matter.

Personal History

A traceable owner history can serve to support the authenticity of the documentation and further bolster pedigree. A full owner history establishes the lineage of that VIN. Remember the cottage industry of VIN stamping? That did not stop at engine blocks and transmission cases. Make sure that you have the one and only car bearing the VIN number found in that database.

Knowing the history of a vehicle back to when it was just a used car (before they were seen by some as cash cows) greatly bolsters that key of authenticity. Even if you are confident about a car's authenticity, it pays dividends to trace it as far back as possible.

Having maintenance history along with receipts can also explain the character of the car. If the car's original owner saw fit to keep meticulous track of its paperwork, then it is just as likely that the car received the same care. There is also an intangible but real value to knowing its story.

It is exciting to see the original dealer brochure marked up by the first owner while he or she made their choices. There is a magic to have spoken to the person behind the name on the original invoice, being part of the unbroken chain of ownership over the years. Being able to learn the stories told by former owners adds to the satisfaction of enjoying a classic muscle car.

Former Owners

If the current owner has not bothered to do the digging, find out as much as possible about the car before buying it. Former owners are more candid and objective about a how a car was repaired and used than any current owner would be.

Scoring systems vary widely from sanctioning body to sanctioning body. When looking at purchasing a restored car or having it judged, begin by understanding how precise the scoring system is and what specific areas on which they focus.

Protect yourself from being passed a hot potato. How many times has an owner bothered to check the numbers on the engine himself? When asked, the owner might simply reply, "The guy I bought it from said the numbers matched." Even fewer call the name and phone number on the original bill of sale, warranty card, or protect-o-plate. If you do, you may be surprised to discover the red Chevelle SS 454 sitting in the garage was a brown Malibu 350 when it sat in his.

It could be worse. They may never have owned such a car, and now it is unclear what you bought. This happens far more often than you would expect.

Some cars that earn big-dollar returns often start as a forlorn barn find, bought for a modest coin and a thank-you from the better half for clearing out the clutter. The person who bothers to do the digging on a car's history is the one who deserves the gold.

Even if the individual history of the car is no more than a line of private owners and a build sheet, it is a better value than owning a saucer full of secrets. A nice, completely unrestored example can be in the garage, but

When it comes to personal history and previous owners, this 1972 Pontiac Grand Prix has it in spades. It is unrestored, rust free, and in Excellent condition. This car was bought new by the current owner's grandfather, owned second by his father, and now him. He is 16, and this is his first car. What a great way to get started in the collector car hobby! If you are also starting out in the hobby and a car like this hasn't been handed down to you from one generation to the next, they are still quite attainable. NADA Classic Price Guide puts the average retail price of this car at $10,050. There were several of these at the Cruisin' Tigers Pontiac Club Indian Uprising car show, where this photo was taken.

without its personal story, the conversation gets short.

Like UFOs, "black box" cars with no documents or history tend to inspire more unanswered questions, breeding suspicion rather than growing joy. These cars also tend not to stay with any one owner very long.

Car collecting is not buying a commodity; it's buying a piece of history. The best buys have their personal history intact.

Condition

While most owners focus on the condition of the car, it is the least important of the five keys of collectability. The other keys cannot be changed or "improved" without undermining the integrity of the entire automobile.

> "While most owners focus on the condition of the car, it is the least important of the five keys of collectability."

Making an engine "more original" by restamping a date code–correct block is frowned upon and is considered fraud in most circles. Fabricating the personal history or factory-original documentation for a vehicle i counterfeiting. Altering or adding to the factory option that a car was originally produced with takes a car out o consideration for OEM concours judging and limits th

Without the mountains of documentation that accompanied this 1970 Chevelle, it would be easy to conclude that it was an up-badged 350 Malibu. Not so. This LS 454 SS was ordered new to be the ultimate sleeper right down to the column shifter and gold brocade interior. The factory fender callouts were the only clue that an unsuspecting stoplight racer was asking for more trouble than he or she could handle.

value—even if it does increase the eye appeal of the car. Creating a clone or tribute vehicle that is a near-perfect replica of an original may boost value compared to a basic model, but it does not make a car suddenly authentic.

Taking a tired original car with good bones and replacing or refurbishing every nut, bolt, and screw on the car—*that* is restoration.

Condition is the only area that collectors and enthusiasts agree can be improved without a negative impact to a collectible car's integrity or authenticity. It is more advantageous to find a well-documented, original sheet metal, original drivetrain vehicle that was desirably optioned and required a complete restoration than to find a car in perfect condition missing any one of the other things. It is even better to buy an older concours restoration and update or refresh it than to purchase a fresh trailer queen that is missing a vital piece of factory

documentation, is difficult to authenticate, or is perhaps not as desirably optioned.

This principle, of course, has its limits. The entirety of the car must be intact. Being a total rust bucket that requires every body panel to be replaced from the frame rails up does not meet the requirements. That would violate the key of originality. Most collectors agree that a car requiring more than 50 percent of its original sheet metal being replaced is a rebody.

Cutting the numbers out of a rusted-out hulk and grafting them onto a clean donor is an "air car," which is also fraudulent. Taking a solid body down to bare metal and rebuilding it with new reproduction materials and reconditioning the main components to like-new condition is restoration. Even with unrestored cars, a limited amount of cleaning, preservation, and remediation of original components can improve the condition of a car

This 1966 GTO convertible shows 99,000 miles on the odometer. It has never been completely restored, only intensively maintained and well cared for. The only clue that this is a high-mileage survivor sits in the engine bay: mismatched colored brackets and flaking paint off the engine block bear witness to a motor that has been personalized, torn down, and rebuilt over the years.

is car rides smoother than many freshly rotisserie restored cars I've driven. I really hope I look this good when I hit y 55th birthday. Before a person just getting into the hobby becomes intimidated by a car of this quality and dis- isses the idea of affording a car like this, check the market. Price guides put the value of a car in this condition any- here from $24,000 on the low end to about $39,000 on average. That is more affordable than the common grocery tter today.

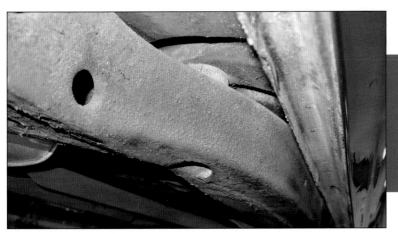

Here is an underbody shot of the same car that spent every year of its life in the western suburbs of Chicago. As you can see, this car never saw salt, and exhaust pipes aside, is remarkably rust free.

Many a young automotive enthusiast would attest to wanting the very car photographed here: the 1968–1970 Corvette Stingray roadster in red. This car is the whole bar stool; it's real, desirable, has the original drivetrain and all the paperwork, and is in Excellent show driver condition. A first-time buyer may not even ask the owner at the show if he would consider selling it because he or she thinks there is no way that it is affordable. That buyer would be passing up a golden opportunity. The current price guide value as of the publishing of this book ranges between $14,300 for the same car needing some TLC and $39,400 for a car in this very condition. The average price for a 1969 L48 Corvette Stingray convertible stands at $24,300. Figure even 10 percent less than that considering the automatic transmission. Passing on the poster car before finding out if it's possible would be a most costly mistake.

without negating its status as an unrestored, surviving example.

Imagine each of these keys is a part of your favorite barstool. The seat is desirability, and the four legs are authenticity, originality, pedigree, and condition. The perfect barstool has a comfy, cushioned seat that fits when you sit on it and is supported by four sturdy legs. You would pay a premium for one that has it all.

Now, picture the stool with three legs. Still good, still sturdy, and the cushion is a great fit. The same holds true with each of these keys. Desirability is superior to any of the other keys that support it. If a vehicle is rare and desirable enough, any one of the three can be less than perfect and still represent a perfectly collectible car.

In general, of the four remaining keys, condition is the leg easiest to bolster or compensate. Specific make nd models differ from this basic formula, and each key is weighted differently among them. That is covered next.

It is easy to fall victim to the false belief that the "perect" collector car is available only to the wealthy and hat this minimum buy-in sits at six figures. That is an ttitude that will blind you to the abundant opportunies you can regularly run into.

If the first-time buyer focuses on all the problems, oadblocks, and automobiles that are out of his or her reach, the person will never see the great ones landing right in his or her path. These principles scale, whether buying a $3,500 car or a $3.5 million car. There are plenty of people with very impressive collections who started by turning wrenches with an affordable classic and kept trading up the chain until they had those six- and seven-figure unicorns sitting in their stable. Pick the highest starting point within your comfort zone and enjoy it. Then, improve it, sell it, and move up from there.

he price guides ding many models, this Corvette included, for having an automatic transmission by 10 percent or nore. We see this as an opportunity for someone just entering the hobby to buy automatic models that are currently ess desirable to the generation that grew up with them. The fact is, most people younger than 35 today probably ave never driven a manual-shift car, let alone prefer one for a performance car. The current generation of Corvette loesn't even offer a stick-shift option. So, if a shifter like this one is sticking out of the console, take the extra 10 per-ent as added upside to the future value of your collector car purchase.

3 USING KEYS TO BUILD A BARSTOOL

The five keys of collectability (desirability, authenticity, originality, pedigree, and condition) are tools for collecting but not a strategy. It's similar to how a measuring cup is a tool for knowing how much of each ingredient is needed but it's not a recipe. Your success in collecting cars is determined by knowing to what degree each key of collectability is for you to build a solid barstool that fits you perfectly.

When looking for a car that holds its value, can be truly enjoyed, and perhaps provide a decent return on the investment, pick any three of the four legs. This provides a solid foundation for collectability.

Not every collector car is collectible for the same reason. While it is true that desirability is superior to the other keys to collectability, each leg looks different depending on the make and model or the intended use of the vehicle.

The interplay between authenticity, originality, pedigree, and condition differs by make and model. For instance, a state-of-the-art Pro Touring car isn't as valuable with the original engine and transmission

A Pro-Touring builder puts its own modern stamp on a car while honoring the original lines of a beloved classic. This is a modern take on the third-generation Dodge Charger R/T. The value of a Pro-Touring collector car is rooted in how modern and powerful the drivetrain is. Does it give the buyer the experience and bragging rights for having the latest technology and the highest advertised horsepower numbers? Additionally, does it give you reliable, low-maintenance speed?

Facing page: Everyone's idea of what a number-one car looks like is different. That is why there is no one-size-fits-all rule for what makes one car more valuable than the other.

This is an original, numbers-matching, surviving 1969 Nova with 13,885 miles on the odometer still owned by its first owner. Every receipt is still with the car. The only category this car fails to log into is pedigree. (Photos Courtesy Diane Eisenschenk)

If the objective is to build a stable of contemporary collectibles, then condition is the most important key for you. This first-generation Chrysler 300C SRT8 showed only 15,000 miles when I sold it for the original owner. It was definitely pampered; it still smelled new.

intact as it is when it is equipped with the latest high-performance drivetrain. It is also much more important for a 1970 Chevelle LS6 to have its original engine intact than it is for a 1971 Hemi 'Cuda.

If the aim is a factory-original piece, authenticity is superior to the other three legs. On most Chevrolet products from the muscle car era, it is nearly impossible to authenticate an original LS6 from a clone without the original motor intact and ideally backed by factory documentation, such as a build sheet.

So, that means originality and pedigree have to play a bigger role in determining the collectability of the Chevelle. The 1971 Hemi 'Cuda, on the other hand, is much

easier to authenticate. Chrysler products from the muscle car era have the engine denoted as a letter within the VIN code, whereas Chevrolets do not.

You can find a 1971 Hemi 'Cuda convertible body shell sitting abandoned in a field on oil drums and restored with a correct but non-VIN-stamped drivetrain, and the investment is protected. That is not a theory, either. One such car sold at the Barrett-Jackson Scottsdale auction for $1.32 million in 2013.

With the LS6, even if the car lived in a heated garage its entire life, without the original drivetrain or original build sheet, there is nothing to tell the prospective buyer if this is indeed a true SS 454 or a 350-powered Malibu.

Facing page: Here is a more detailed look at the sleeper LS6 Chevelle SS. This car is well documented as an authentic 454 SS. Having the original engine is so intrinsic to the authenticity of the car that it also impacts the value of the vehicle more significantly than with other makers.

Some other manufacturers have extensive production databases that can tell exactly how the car was originally equipped. So, it is much easier to authenticate a highly desirable vehicle if it is backed by a factory database.

Original documentation and even original components become less important legs to the stool. Each make and marque has its own standards of authenticity. As a collector, it is important to become familiar with them to make certain that the genuine article is being bought and not a convincing fraud.

Even if it can be proven that a car is authentic without it being particularly original or possessing a perfect pedigree, these factors can become more important given the intended use for the vehicle. If you are looking for an over-the-top restored car to show on the International Show Car Association (ISCA) circuit over a like-new modern classic with ultra-low miles, condition is the primary driver of collectability.

If the low-mile modern classic is the target, then originality and pedigree follow right behind. A clean Car Fax and maintenance records that prove an owner's claim that the car has been well cared for and is still in original paint is key. If the custom show car is the goal, then neither of those factors are important. Pedigree becomes more about who built a car and what awards it has won on the show circuit to support the awesome condition the car is in.

If you are looking for a regional show car, one that can be driven without driving the value out of it, condition is less critical. There's no sense paying for highly polished floor pans just to pick up rock chips speeding down a stretch of Route 66. If you plan to drive the car often, it makes more sense to pick a car that is desirable and authentic but perhaps does not have the original motor. The purchase is more affordable on the front end by about 10 percent compared to the

This 1969 Dodge Hemi Daytona's early life as an ISCA show car was instrumental to its preservation. While this obviously is not its original paint job, it did retain all its original sheet metal, interior, and drivetrain.

Here is that 1969 Hemi Daytona again, restored to factory-original specifications. Of the 503 Daytonas Dodge produced in 1969, only 22 were equipped with a 426 Hemi engine and backed by a 4-speed manual transmission as this one was. It is also only one of a handful that is documented by an original broadcast sheet and still has its original Hemi engine. When cars like these have all five keys, bring the checkbook because it just becomes a battle of who wants it more.

same car equipped with the original engine (more like 25 percent or more for the vintage Chevy), and if the engine does get hurt, the originality is not diminished any further.

If an unrestored car that has survived in its original state for the last 50 years is the aim, then originality is just as important as authenticity. Condition follows closely behind. The more intact and the better the shape the car is in all areas (interior, engine bay, exterior body, and chassis), the more invaluable the car becomes.

Pedigree plays a secondary role here. Paperwork can be sparse for cars of this age, but a benchmark original example speaks for itself. Of course, if the car also has a full complement of factory-original paperwork, it becomes an elite collectible and the price becomes inestimable.

These aren't all the manners in which collector cars

are used and enjoyed, but they provide a framework of how the five keys to collectability can be used. The unique features inherent in a given make and marque should be taken into consideration together with the buyer's collecting objectives.

Once it is understood how these factors work together, a solid automotive investment can be made. If a car is missing more than one of these keys, unless rarity and desirability are astronomically high, you are likely looking at more of a toy than an investment-quality collector's item.

Of course, if you need to have it all (a car that is eminently desirable, 100-percent original, undeniably authentic, has a pedigree complete back to the first owner, and is in benchmark quality condition), you will need a blank-check budget and be willing to pay whatever it takes to own it. So will the next person if you decide to sell it.

4 SOURCING: LOOKING FOR THE RIGHT CAR IN ALL THE WRONG PLACES

The advent of the smartphone, social media, and 24/7 connectivity has produced the illusion that the rare is readily accessible. For commodities, the world is certainly at your fingertips. That includes high-volume, high-performance joy toys. Thousands of photos and videos of some of the rarest and most remarkable vehicles on the planet can be found online, but that does not mean they can be bought as easily. It is like looking at the ocean through a keyhole and being unable to buy a bottle of Dasani.

Part of beginning with the end in mind is making certain to look for a target vehicle in the right place. You would not go searching for crocodiles in Alaska or fishing for yellow-fin tuna in Lake Michigan. It is frustrating to sort through all the tired grocery getters on Craigslist or hacked-together project cars on eBay Motors to find "the one." Perhaps "the one" is not so elusive; you are just fishing in the wrong pond or need to cast off the other side of the boat. The problem is deciding which strategy should be employed.

You may see the car of your dreams pretty much everywhere: your social media feed, favorite car magazines, online content providers, or auction coverage on TV. But you're also continuously frustrated when looking for one you can actually purchase.

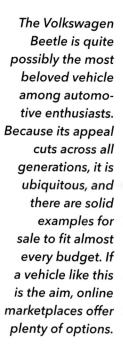

The Volkswagen Beetle is quite possibly the most beloved vehicle among automotive enthusiasts. Because its appeal cuts across all generations, it is ubiquitous, and there are solid examples for sale to fit almost every budget. If a vehicle like this is the aim, online marketplaces offer plenty of options.

Sourcing Plan

For vehicles like project cars, daily drivers, or even seasonal drivers, browsing online advertising channels (Craigslist, eBay Motors, and Facebook Marketplace) may be good places to include in a sourcing plan. Include some of the high-volume classic car dealerships in the search as well as classified ad websites that specialize in classic cars. However, be prepared to do a lot of qualifying and eliminating of purchase candidates before creating a short list. Do the due diligence or perhaps even go see it in person.

That is the nature of that end of the market. It's not unlike keeping a restaurant fully staffed with competent, reliable people. It is a perpetual process. So, if you are looking for a 10-year-old Jeep that hasn't been modified or beaten within an inch of its life to play with on weekends and there is no urgency as to when you stumble upon it, then great, burn some time slogging through the listings. If you miss one, they are like a bus, another one will come along. That becomes a hobby all on its own.

The more specialized, rare, and high quality the target vehicle is, the more unlikely it is that you will find it through mass-market advertising. When looking for competitive show cars, private museum pieces, public museum pieces, or concours trailer queens, a much more deliberate and comprehensive approach is needed. It becomes more of a strategy of developing a network of relationships than it does being persistent or even efficient with searching publicly advertised vehicles for sale.

"The more specialized, rare, and high quality the target vehicle is, the more unlikely it is that you will find it through mass-market advertising."

When to Go It Alone versus a Time Crunch

If looking for a limited-production car that is not exactly scarce and the timetable to purchase is relaxed, take the time to develop a network within that community. Join as many clubs and groups as you have time to spend and get to know the actors within that space.

Go to live car shows and get to know current owners of the same car you are hoping to own one day. As

For the average hobbyist, owning a collectible car is not a method of financial planning so much as it is an investment in time. It is a lifestyle, if done correctly, that can be enjoyed for years, and sold for the same or more money than you paid in. You may find that next car at the regional car show or local cruise-in, just by spending your time the way you would anyhow. Just be prepared and informed well enough to take advantage of an opportunity when it presents itself.

elationships develop within this group, an army of spies will also develop to help keep an eye out for the car of your dreams before anyone else finds out about it. Learn those critical data points to plug into the five keys so that when it comes time to validate the new discovery, you know exactly what to look for, what questions to ask, and which trade-offs to weigh.

If you have not spent decades developing relationships in the hobby, your time is more valuably spent working than hanging out in social media chatrooms. If you are on a tight time frame (for example, if it is January and you want to be driving this spring), perhaps it is best to hire a professional to find the right car and avoid costly purchase mistakes. If the target car is a four-legged barstool and only a few dozen were made 50 years ago, sourcing it yourself may result in a very costly object lesson.

The other place that provides the illusion of access and immediacy to rare and remarkable vehicles are live automotive auctions. These auctions have developed a culture within the car hobby. It may be tempting to presume that, nowadays, a unicorn can be bought from a vending machine. While that will never be the case, there are circumstances where it makes sense to wade into the deep end, swim with the sharks, and come back with the trophy and one hell of a story.

When Paying a Professional Pays Off

Nothing sucks the fun out of a lifelong pursuit of the car of your dreams like the countless hours spent scrolling through pages and pages of second-rate cars or fluffed-up junk in search of "the one." What's worse is talking to a seller halfway across the continent and getting on an airplane only to find that it is nothing, *nothing* like it was described.

The fact is that most private collectors are just that: private. Most of the time, they don't flaunt their cars publicly on Facebook. At best, good cars, cruisers, toys, or projects are found being shown off by owners in groups like a never-ending virtual swap meet.

Most people selling on social media are dealers or flippers who are always looking to turn a car over quickly. The rarest of the rare, the best of the best, keep their cars close to the vest. If they feature them on social media, it is usually a picture collector, a professional media outfit, or an organized car show featuring the car, with no direct link to the owner. A good broker has already cultivated a community of reputable enthusiasts specializing in the type of vehicles you are targeting. They will have direct contact with (or at least be one degree of separation from) the car you are looking for.

They also know the correct places to search online

Cars like this multi-carbureted Challenger are often not advertised or publicly offered for sale. A professional inspection confirmed that this one was rotisserie restored with the original drivetrain intact. Some of the most impressive cars move just like this, quietly through private brokers.

and in the real world to expand their search beyond their sphere of influence. Beware, if a person claiming to know "where all the cars are hidden" is presenting cars found through classified-ad websites, online auctions, and dealers' digital showrooms, they aren't a professional broker; they are just another keyboard cowboy looking to turn a quick buck without offering much value.

Selection and Inspection

It doesn't serve much of a purpose to load a buyer with more options that aren't a good match. It wastes time instead of saving it. Perhaps the calculation is that they can sell something lesser if everything seems mediocre. Buyers didn't get to the point of buying a classic or building a collection by settling.

A full-service broker not only knows where to find cars that are off the beaten path or out of the public eye, but they also know how to quickly determine whether the prospective purchase is a good fit for the buyer. The

This 2002 Ford F150 Harley-Davidson Edition has only 5,000 miles. The owner first offered this limited-edition truck in 2012 for $26,500, only attracting a low-ball buyer. Instead of selling it short, he decided to hold on to it for a while. It was offered for sale again in 2020, this time earning $51,700. A smart move for the seller and a bad move for the first potential buyer for overplaying his hand.

ey here is securing the right information instead of
alling back on a rote series of questions that may end
p having a buyer pass on the right car for the wrong
easons.

By the time a broker presents a car, the preliminary
ue diligence should be done. This includes leveraging
heir own trusted network of marque experts to make sure
he car is as described by the owner. If a buyer decides to
nove forward to making an offer on the car, the broker
ill then coordinate an independent, third-party inspecion to verify the car is as represented.

Fees for these services range from broker to broker
nd within each market segment. Most full-service bro-
ers charge a percentage of the agreed sales price of the
ehicle. Typically, those who are acting merely as bird
ogs, feeding their clients unqualified leads, charge about
 to 3 percent. A full-service broker earns about 6 to 10
ercent, depending upon his or her range of services and
epth of expertise.

Other brokers charge a flat fee per car for their ser-
ice. This is more common if they are acting as a buyer's

representative, simply inspecting the car and facilitating
the transaction. In any case, these services performed
correctly quickly pay for themselves in well-negotiated
sales of well-qualified cars.

Negotiation and Acquisition

The art of negotiation comes down to emotional
detachment. Emotional entanglement with the car (or
more precisely what the car stands for) is the very thing
that high-pressure sales environments such as auctions
rely upon to get a buyer to pay the most (or more) than
he or she is willing to spend.

> **"The art of negotiation comes down to emotional detachment."**

When acting as a buyer's agent, a professional broker's objective is to find out what is the least amount

*he agreed sale price for any custom or collector car isn't strictly about the price. The terms of sale and the details of
vhat is included are just as important. For a custom car like this, full build receipts and vendor information for all the
najor components are a must. Also important are operating and maintenance instructions. These things make the
difference between owning a cool custom or a real mystery machine.*

If a buyer is new to the hobby and in the hunt for a 1971 'Cuda but doesn't have the big dollars to throw at a Hemi or 440+6 car, alternatives like this 1971 Plymouth 'Cuda 340 4-speed or a 383 are also collectible. They are also more enjoyable to drive every day when compared to their big-block brothers.

The connections a good broker has aren't limited to sourcing good cars, it is about all the other referral relationships and vendor partners. A buyer can find the car of a lifetime and still have disappointment delivered by picking the wrong provider.

the owner will take. This is a listening skill that require being interested in the car but not excited about th idea of owning it. What is exciting to the broker whil negotiating is finding out what the primary motivatior is behind the sale and what elements of the deal can b influenced to bring the price down as low as possible fo the benefit of the buyer.

Often, what motivates the seller to commit to a sale agreement does not have to do with price at all. The pos ture is one of always being willing to walk away, no mat ter how good a fit the car may otherwise seem. If th terms of the sale aren't right, then the car isn't either Next.

Closing and Clearing the Deal

Once a broker has secured an agreement with th seller, he or she should also have a standard process witl which to guide the buyer and the seller through to ensur a smooth transition of money for goods. Purchasing ar investment-quality collector car is more akin to buying a new home than it is a used car. When transactions are performed remotely and parties are thousands of miles apart, simply meeting up to trade the car and the title for cash and writing out the bill of sale on the back of a Wendy's receipt is no longer practical or even preferable.

All the elements of the deal should be clearly outlined in writing and signed by both parties. The professional broker will have well-drafted deposit and purchase agreements as well as act as an intermediary between both parties to trade cash for title. The broker ensures that everything included in the sale, such as factory documents, previous owner receipts, any related spares, along with any other contingent conditions, are met before the deal is finalized.

If the deal should fail any of the agreed upon contingencies or should either party fail to perform against the agreement, the broker will step in to moderate a satisfactory conclusion of the deal.

Getting the Car Home Safely

Another advantage to hiring a broker is his or her assistance with the other headaches associated with the sale: getting the car home safely. This is one of the biggest challenges to deal with.

Experience is once again key to making certain that the new acquisition arrives safe and sound and in exactly the same condition as it left the seller. Among the many relationships a broker develops and maintains over time, chief among them is a network of reputable and reliable transporters.

An amateur buyer may move one or two cars a year. A professional broker will have coordinated the transport of dozens (if not hundreds) of cars both nationally and internationally and be well versed in the best vendors and procedures given the situation. It is another headache to outsource and another aspect that can provide peace of mind.

A Wealth of Resources Before, During, and After the Sale

A bird dog exits the sale once an introduction between the buyer and the seller is made, sticking around only long enough to make sure he or she gets paid. A used car salesman sticks around long enough for the sales agreement to be signed and the check to clear. A good broker is a constant resource for anything related to the collector car hobby—both directly related to the sale or anything else the buyer may need for his or her collection.

Brokers have a lifetime of resources and experience—use them to your advantage. The good ones always want to add value to your experience and relationship before, during, and after the sale. As I tell all my clients, "This

In-person car shows, such as the Muscle Car and Corvette Nationals, are a great place to put faces to names you may only know on the phone or social media. This is where I spend most of my time, gladly answering people's questions about their cars, their collections, or market trends in general.

By the end of the first phone call with me, you'll hear me say this and know it's true: This isn't about selling a single car, this is about building a lifelong relationship. Here is one of my best clients celebrating concours judging results for the shaker-hood Hemi behind him.

isn't about selling a single car, this is about building a lifelong relationship."

Here are five key questions to ask before engaging any broker.

1. How are your fees structured? Are you paid by both parties or just myself?
2. How do you ensure that the vehicle is legally owned with a negotiable title by the seller?
3. What is your process to ensure that the vehicle is as it is represented and that the transaction is securely completed?
4. What, if any, recourse would I have if the car is delivered and discovered to be materially misrepresented?
5. What is your background and expertise with the type of car I am shopping for?

This 1968 Mustang convertible is one attractive car. Cars like these will often be seen at live auctions, and the auction houses put a "value range" on them to bracket your bidding above the owner's reserve to ensure a sale. The challenge is knowing what it is genuinely worth. The price guide range on a car like this is anywhere from $18,900 for a garage find to $49,800 for a trailer queen. It is important to have a trusted third party that can perform an on-site inspection and appraisal, so know ahead of time if the car has any costly issues and where to set your bid limit. That is a wise strategy for buying a car from any source.

These are just some of the benefits of having a knowledgeable professional in your corner when you are active in the collector car hobby. Even as you build your own expertise and base of contacts, the relationship with the right broker pays dividends over the cost of services over time.

Conflicts of Interest: How to Avoid Being Taken Advantage Of

I've outlined many of the ways that having an expert, professional, objective, and independent actor in your corner is beneficial. It would be a mistake to see everyone who offers help as being interested in serving your needs first. That is how it is supposed to work in business: discover and fulfill the needs of the customer. Do that well and your business will be automatically taken care of.

There are far too many in the classic car industry who just don't see it that way, so pay attention before trusting someone implicitly. Outlining all the ways to be taken advantage of could be a book of its own. As it relates to the purchase and sale of vehicles, the one item that must be known is how the broker or inspector gets paid.

Dual Agency

If a broker is offering services, the only way that he or she gets paid should be when the broker delivers your desired results. If the broker double dips and charges a commission to both the seller and the buyer as is done at auction houses, that is called dual agency. It is unethical at best.

If a problem crops up during such a deal, it is not clear who a dual-agency broker really works for. Instead of mediating an issue for your benefit, this type of broker will most likely work to cover his or her own exposure, leaving both buyer and seller in the lurch. In real estate, dual agency is illegal specifically for this reason.

There can be other pitfalls when working with an unscrupulous broker. The most important thing to look out for is potential conflicts of interest. Be sure the broker draws clear boundaries and that his or her process demonstrates that the broker is working for you and not taking advantage of you.

Paying a Broker

Another major conflict of interest to be aware of and avoid occurs when hiring a subject matter expert or a professional inspector. How do they get paid? Most charge a simple flat fee for service, and if that is the extent of it, they can perhaps be trusted to be objective and provide unbiased information.

If the inspector derives the majority of his or her income from a different source, then be aware that a conflict of interest exists and perhaps choose a provider hat does not have any compromising entanglements. 'or instance, if the person hired to authenticate a potential purchase also brokers cars or is paid a commission to ocate them for an already-established client base, you nay be exposing yourself to becoming the bird dog for a ompetitor also building his collection.

I have witnessed many instances when a third-party nspector turned in a less-than-favorable review on an nspection, only to later find that they brokered it to omeone else. I have also seen people position themselves s the ultimate authority, the imprimatur of authenticity, or a given make or marque only to discover that their usiness model derives most of its income from consigning vehicles to an auction house.

So, make sure the inspector is here to evaluate a rospective purchase for you and parts for your current ollection—not to solicit consignments as an outside alesperson for his or her primary clients, a group of aucion houses. Motive matters.

This goes back to the very dawn of classic car dealerhips that offer "free appraisals" to fish for new inventory. nother age-old goody is the restoration shop owner who lso offers low-cost prepurchase inspections but every car eems to fail to meet his or her standard and can only be nade right if he or she had the opportunity to restore it.

Too many good cars have been passed on because the erson being relied on to make sense out of the buyer's nterests first and foremost provided biased or self-serving nformation instead of objective facts uncompromised y an ulterior motive. Instead of making sense of the car

for you, he or she found a way to enrich himself/herself. Beware and be sure to get the right help.

Auction Houses: How to Turn the Tables

The possibility of getting a great collectible car is the allure that draws thousands to the auction tent every year. Although, when attending an auction for the first time, it can be difficult to see all of the variables that can affect the outcome of the event and a potential purchase. You walk into the bidding arena with the VIP pass around your neck where the stage is set, the red carpets are laid down, and the lights are dazzling.

The energy of the circus tent and buzz from the bleachers brings goosebumps. The chrome is gleaming, and the collector cars are waxed to a mirror finish and perhaps looking the best they ever have behind the velvet rope. These and other aspects can determine whether you end up with an incredible car for a paltry price or a tremendous case of heartburn at the end of the day. That is why it is critical to draw a battle strategy beforehand.

Why Is This Car There?

Understand the nature of the environment. Auctions tend to be high-volume, low-probability places to find a high-quality car. Yes, the "featured collection" may contain some pieces of merit, but that is about a dozen out of 3,000 or more cars offered on a given weekend. Most of those are dealers sending cars they could not sell for retail on the regular market when buyers can take their

Not everything that glitters under the auction lights is gold. It is easy to get caught up in the excitement of the auction environment, especially as a first-time buyer. When entering an auction, keep in mind that you are buying the car and not buying into the auction environment.

The staging lanes at an auction are a great place to visit with friends, trade speculative guesses as to what this one will go for, and perhaps make some new acquaintances. The moment right before the car rolls onto the block is the wrong time to begin performing due diligence on a target vehicle. Homework should have been completed weeks before the auction began.

time, do their due diligence, and carefully inspect a vehicle before committing to purchase.

"Auctions tend to be high-volume, low-probability places to find a high-quality car."

Others make a living off building vehicles on spec to sell at auction. Purchasing a spec car that was built on a budget to ensure a profit and constrained by the timetable to make certain it is ready and on time for the auction event is much different than buying a car from a private owner who personally commissioned it.

The owner paid time and materials over a year or more to make sure their personal vision was actualized. Sometimes there are marketable cars that roll across the block, and that makes all the hassle involved in going to the auction and making a bid worth it. It is not like flying in for a party. It is more like planning a high-adventure camping trip in the jungle. Expect it to be fun, or it can be truly dangerous if you are ill-equipped or ill-prepared.

Auction Preparation

Weeks in advance of attending an auction, it is important to do your homework. As in the art of war, a good general gets scouting reports and reviews the plan of attack. In advance of going into action at an auction,

carefully consider what type of car you are trying to buy and the ultimate purpose of that car.

In addition, take a candid inventory of both what you know and do not know about making an educated purchase. The ability to prepare and the willingness to walk away from the wrong situation can determine success or failure. You are on a conquest and everyone else with a bidder's pass or a seller's slip is the adversary. Even the auction house is a fortress of divided loyalty.

"As an auction house, we are in an interesting position," said Dana Mecum, owner of Mecum Auction Inc. "We are there to get the seller the best price (for his car) and also want the buyer to feel he [or she] got a fair deal."

The Calculations

The desire for the car of your dreams may push you to compromise on quality. Do not do it. Know the conditions of satisfaction and stick to them.

Sharpen your pencil on the budget as well. Learn the market value for the car by studying the published results from previous auctions for similar cars. Talk to those in the club community about the direction of values and find out what similar cars have recently sold for privately. Sometimes the prices achieved at auctions have little to do with the merits of a car. Sometimes the prices reflect a quality of car poorer than you are willing to accept.

If the market seems too high in general for what you can comfortably afford, and you are really itching to buy something, consider the possibility that perhaps an

The entire auction environment is focused on this moment, which lasts about 3 minutes. It is designed to make attendees feel like they are getting a good deal, flooding the senses and stroking the competitive ego to make sure they pay the very most that can be mustered in that moment of temporary time pressure.

The reserve is off! This 1970 Mercury Cougar Boss 302 Eliminator is a rare one. Sold in 2015, this is one of only two in Competition Blue and equipped with a Super Drag Pak option. The price guide value for this car prior to the event was about $75,000. The excitement of being part of the featured collection on television prime time likely explains the $195,000 price tag.

auction is not the best place to buy. Mecum offers this bit of reality testing: "Auctions are built on excitement. A new buyer can get caught up in that excitement and bid more than expected."

Likewise, giving too much on quality standards to fit a price point for purchase can cost much more in the long run. Even buying a car that has not been advertised that needs a little TLC out of a private collection may be more affordable than one effectively promoted at auction.

Practice Swings

It is also a good idea to survey the surroundings. One veteran auction buyer recommended to first attend a few of the auctions run by the same auction house you intend to use without registering to bid. This approach provides a sober prospective of the environment like that general getting a good feel for the battlefield.

Note how the ringmen work the bidders and how the lights and the show stage affect the appearance of the car

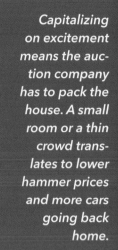

Capitalizing on excitement means the auction company has to pack the house. A small room or a thin crowd translates to lower hammer prices and more cars going back home.

It is exciting to see bread-and-butter cars like this 1970 383 Road Runner in such clean original condition. Every once in a while, it is possible to talk with the owner of the car. That is a tremendous opportunity to confirm the information gathered in your research and fill in some of the blanks remaining in your homework.

compared to how it looks waiting in the corral.

Pay attention to what times of day the bidders' area is less crowded. Target opportunity buys that roll across the block during these lulls. The gallery often empties out around lunch or right after some featured showcase cars run across the block. Auction prime time used to be a late-night affair. The advent of auctions as television entertainment and an aging buying base means that some great buys can be had after dinner time, even on a Friday or a Saturday night. Fewer adversaries to bid against means a better gavel price.

Look at some of the more subjective aspects too. Is

free alcohol served to the bidders? Remember to stick to bottled water the day of bidding. Also look for weaknesses in the environment. Does the auction house tend to take on many last-minute consignments? This is indicated by the number of lots that end in a decimal point, (e.g., 101.1). Does the auction house tend to run on schedule or run behind?

Early consignments do not get advanced promotion that draw people intending to bid on a specific car. Last-minute additions rely on incidental traffic and are at the mercy of the environment. If overall attendance is low or too many of the same model show up, the last-minute car could be an incredibly good buy. Take advantage of the seller's lack of planning by being prepared to evaluate these cars on-site. Last-minute additions and late-running lots can take less-observant bidders off guard, leaving you to reap the reward of a well-bought beauty.

Take the time to assess the competition. Do the same faces show up auction after auction? Make note of what they bid on, their bidding habits, if they always gravitate to the same ringman, or if they maintain eye contact directly with the auctioneer, etc.

Mock Bid

Practice bidding on paper, see where you end up compared to those placing live bids. This helps build confidence and intuition. If you end up competing with more experienced bidders for the same car down the road, you will be prepared to adjust your strategy accordingly.

Continued Research

After surveying the playing field and assessing the potential competition, take time to crystallize the vision of your mission objective. Do the research needed to really assess the knock-out factors to decide if a specific car is right to bid on or if it is a particular make or model you are targeting.

For instance, if you are looking for a 1969½ lift-off-hood Road Runner, know where all the body numbers appear on the car, what the special notches look like on the front fenders, what the stamp pad codes for a six-pack block are compared to a standard 440 engine block, and what typically came on an A-12 packaged car. Also, know what options typically appeared on the fender tag, how many still have the original motor, how to tell if the date codes on the intake and carburetors are also original to the car, how to tell if the lift-off hood is original or reproduction, how to check the A-12 registry to get a history, etc. As your buying objective progress gets closer to buying a concours-quality investment car, the more detailed your research needs to be.

For a specific car, use club contacts, network relationships, and online discussion boards to trace the owner, any history, and the background on that individual lot.

The value of any collectible car can hinge on the presence or absence of key equipment. For the Boss 302 engine bay, these include the smog, air cleaner snorkel, S tube, and rev limiter. If things such as these are missing, they may be expensive to buy or hard to find. Learn what those items are for the car you are targeting.

Auction catalog photos look, well, like catalog models. That photography is designed to entice, not document. Once at the auction venue, what you find may shock you. The cracking on the fender of this 1967 Corvette is shocking close up and completely invisible on a picture taken 10 feet away.

Use this information to set a bidding threshold and as a comparison to how the car presents during the auction event.

If targeting more than one car of the same make or just fishing for a good deal, use those same resources to learn what things typically are missing, incorrect, or wear out first, such as a 1970 Boss 302 missing its snorkel, S tube, and rev limiter.

Evaluate the Car for Neglect

Become familiar with signs of abuse or masked abuse. A front radiator support that has been replaced is a sign of front-end damage. Overspray on door seals or a rear valance that has been mudded in may point to hasty bodywork.

Look at the frame rails and the inner fender aprons for evidence of welded-in patches or outright replacement. An engine bay could be missing thousands in original smog, air cleaner, and performance equipment. Sometimes an original block has been swapped out for a more common later-model short-block or one cast for use in a truck. If any of these things are detected, be prepared to walk away if originality is your primary criteria.

Acknowledge Limitations

In either case, if your knowledge is limited, bring someone along or hire a professional inspector who is well versed with that particular make to do the evalua-

tion. Acknowledging your limitations can be a strength just as a good general relies on skilled officers for input and advice. Your pocketbook will thank you later. The more homework you do, the more likely your success will be.

Estimate the Costs

When preparing for the main event, do some soul searching by asking yourself, "Am I going to enjoy myself if I invest the time and trouble to learn the auction environment, research the vehicles, and take the necessary time to work the auction to my advantage?" If the answer is no, even if you don't come home with something, you may be setting yourself up for a bad purchase decision.

The environment of an auto auction can be glitzy, relaxed, or even take on a casino atmosphere. Mecum provides this valuable reminder: "When you are buying a car at auction, you are conducting a piece of business."

In other words, keep a detached, businesslike viewpoint to avoid pitfalls. As much as possible, leave emotional attachments at the door. This environment builds a sense of urgency and a scarcity mentality. Keep that influence out and keep in mind that there will always be another car to be had elsewhere. Compare how you approach other major purchases, such as real estate or stock investments, and use those here.

When thinking with the heart rather than the head, let the buyer beware. Record prices set at auction are made by getting caught up in a grudge match with another buyer, rather than the intrinsic value of the automobile. These prices are seldom reinforced by the private market. Unless you are determined to buy a verifiable "one of

Save the Children and other charitable overtures at auctions are designed to establish the house as a benevolent actor, create a feel-good moment, and develop an atmosphere of abundance among the pool of bidders. It also provides a very public tax write-off opportunity for those bidding on charity lots.

one" super car and have the war chest to go belly to belly with the big boys, set a hardline limit and stick to it. Keeping your cool is profit in your pocket.

Additional Costs

Count all the hard costs end to end, including the research, the inspections, the buyer's premium, the transport costs, and the sales tax. Then, compare that total cost to the market research you conducted.

Research

This includes time personally spent or money spent paying someone else to spend their time looking into the background of the vehicle. The internet is an ocean of information. Entering the VIN into the search bar may bring up some institutional memory of the car. There are also registries, web resources, and networking with subject matter experts for many makes and marques which can tell a more complete story about the target car than the catalog entry. This can take hours or 10s of hours. As a rough estimate, a thorough research can cost anywhere from $250 to $1,000 or more.

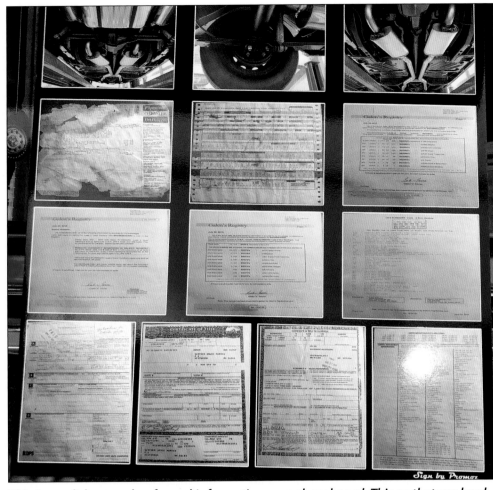

This is a solid example of good information on a show board. Things that are hard to see, the undercarriage detail, and the factory paperwork are all laid out on one visual field. Before bidding, go to the property room and verify that the originals are present and accounted for. Showing all the body and drivetrain VIN stamps would have made this board even better.

Inspection

This is for on-site inspection of a vehicle to confirm condition, detect any concealed problems, and possibly verify how original, correct, or authentic the target vehicle is when compared to the auction representation. This too can range widely from $400 for a cursory inspection to $1,500 or more for a complete visual inspection by an acknowledged expert.

Buyer's Premium

This is the auction house's way of doubling its commission. It charges the seller a commission for selling the car, which is anywhere from 6 to 10 percent. Then, it charges the buyer a similar commission, which is typically 8 to 12 percent. The buyer pays both because the owner sets the reserve to cover his or her end of the cost.

Transport

Once a car is purchased, the buyer must get it home. Prices vary from carrier to carrier per mile and by the distance traveled. As a general range, it is common to spend $1,500 to $2,500 for enclosed door-to-door transport.

Sales Tax

Yes, buying from an auction house is the same as buying from a dealership. Sales tax is collected at the rate established within the state. Depending upon the laws within your home state, private sales aren't taxed at the same rate or are not subject to tax at all. Before buying at an auction house, become familiar with the tax rules in both the state where the auction is being held and those within the state it will be registered. It could mean the difference between paying an additional 8 percent on top of all the other expenses or owing nothing at all.

If the car is in a worse-than-anticipated condition,

This is the best seat in the house. There are clear sight lines to the auctioneer, to the bidding status board, and of the lot. Watch the auctioneer's gestures and be sure to know now where the other bids are coming from. Remain situationally aware.

add the projected cost of repair to the matrix. Divide the hard costs by your return horizon. If the plan is to sell the car within the year, the costs of transaction factor greatly, so keep the bid limit low and seek out opportunity buys. On the other hand, if this is a purchase that will be kept for 5 to 10 years, some of these costs factor minimally.

Avoid the prospect of borrowing heavily to stretch into the car you really want. The boom-and-bust cycle of the collector car market is due in part to people literally betting the ranch to get in on the auction action, anticipating they will make a killing at the same venue next year. Most of the time, they later need to dump the car at a loss while the auction house earns money twice. Do the math and decide the best limit for you.

Plan the Attack

Show up early. Showing up a few days before bidding opens provides access to everything that is needed to make a proper assessment of the car. Visit the property room and review all of its paperwork. If possible, gain direct access to the owner and interview him or her about the car. Remember, that little card read by the auctioneer is provided by the person selling the car—not an objective inspector with an expert eye.

Whenever possible, personally talk to the owner (or owner's representative) on the day the car arrives. Make note of any glaring differences between the catalog write-up and your personal assessment. This is a tremendous opportunity to inspect the car before it is in show-car detail and discover the seller's state of mind.

For instance, try to find out what is motivating the sale. Determine if the seller needs to sell it, if it is reasonably priced but he or she is happy to take it back home, or if he or she is just there to test the limits of the market.

Give enough time to double-check your homework and complete your research. Run the VIN through a collector registry or other resource. If you are not expert enough to trust your own eyes, take photos and send them to someone who is.

Find out when the car is set to roll across the block, double-check the weather, and find out who else seems to be checking out the car and listen intently. Once the car is fully examined and the competition is surveyed, set a bid limit and position yourself for the purchase.

Some auctions combine the hype man and barker positions. Here, we have the hype man out front, tasked with talking up each car and emceeing the event, keeping energy in the room high. The best way to avoid being swept up in the barker's rap is to not open the bid. Let someone else take the hit of falling in too high.

Positioning and Directing

Select a seat in the front few rows with an unobstructed view of the auctioneer. Keep track of the auction results, the schedule, and the mood of the other bidders. A win here looks like getting the car for the bid limit (or less) or walking away without getting sucked into the game. In this position, there is no defeat.

When looking around, note the other bidders with a ringman next to them. It is the ringman's job to find out who is a prospect on the car and communicate that to the auctioneer. That way, the auctioneer knows there is good competition and can keep the car on the block longer until someone raises his or her hand.

The auctioneer opens the bid by barking out a suggested price. This is an illusion. If the auctioneer does not know who the players are on the car until a bid is placed, there is the illusion that there are fewer bidders interested in the car. Listen to the auctioneer who is dropping that suggested price until someone "falls into the bid." By not paying attention to the ringmen and other buyers, a buyer can fall into the bid too high and dash all hopes of ending up with their price.

The lower the opening bid, the shorter the gavel, the fewer the competitors. If this is a car you want, you want it on the block for as short of a time as possible. When the auctioneer says, "Somebody give me a starting price," the car is likely to be a bargain. At this point, people may begin inspecting the car for the first time, attempting to quickly assess a potential steal too late. Competitors who have not researched the car as thoroughly can be scared off by such a low opening bid.

Even if it is low, do not be the one to open the bid. A short gavel may also force the seller to drop his reserve if there is one, thinking it may spur bidding. They usually sell well short of market value when that happens.

Go Ahead, Take Advantage

There are times when the auction environment shows its weakness. These are things that the auction house cannot control, such as the elements. Bad weather can chase away a few bidding competitors.

Sometimes, an auction house has consigned too many of the same type of car. More choice with a limited audience means a buying opportunity. If the house has taken on an excess of last-minute consignments (those decimal point lots mentioned earlier), there may be a good car that has not been properly promoted. An abundance of late entries can also mean a crowded schedule that results in shorter block times. These situations may prove to be an advantage if the lots are rushed. As noted already, the shorter the time the car is on the block, the better it is for the buyer.

For all the power the auction environment wields, it has no power over the weather. Poor weather can result in low turnouts or worse. A severe storm hit this auction site in January 2010 and collapsed two tents that were housing cars. The next day, it was a scratch-and-dent sale. Those who had to sell let their cars go for pennies on the dollar.

Poorly promoted lots not cataloged in advance result in fewer rival bidders. Featured premium lots can run late into the evening, thinning the bidding pool. Keep track of the position of your target lot. Many a bidder has been caught off guard, missing an opportunity because he or she has not kept track.

"At any auction, even when you set world records, there are always cars that sell under value," Mecum observes.

When the seller (and other bidders) fails to prepare appropriately, he or she gives the buyer the advantage.

Sellers may show up at the last minute with good cars that have a poor detail job, a bad battery, and a stale tank of gas. This shortfall has produced an entire breed of flippers who specialize in buying them. These quick-buy artists know that $200 worth of failed prep can mean saving as much as $15,000 on the auction block. Give these resale specialists a little pushback when bidding, and you could end up with a good car with plenty of value left over.

On the other hand, it is also important to recognize when the auction environment is the strongest. The auction lots that received the most exposure (usually found on the cover of the auction handout) bring out the big-money players and sometimes the TV cameras. This is a good time for the average Joe to sit on his or her hands. Be there to buy a car, not bid for 15 minutes of fame.

The Fiery Attack

Be the "new money." The person who opens the bid is rarely the bidder who ends up with the car. If that

"Fail to prepare and prepare to fail" is how the saying goes. The engine is the jewel. The car is the jewelry box. This looks like the owner forgot to polish the diamond or even burnish the manure. He will pay dearly on the block for saving a few dollars on clean up and correction. This model of Mustang did come with air conditioning, a major blow to the car's value and collectability. However, if bought right, it is a tremendous opportunity to own. It can always be corrected to enhance the resale value down the road.

person does, he or she probably paid every penny and then some. Wait until they are just about to put the hammer down before placing your first bid. The auctioneer will utter excitedly, "New money!"

By this time, opponents have either bid their limit

Auctioneering is about controlling pace and keeping energy high. Jump in when the call is to your advantage. If the air is let out of the room and the auctioneer is groping for the next bid and seems to be about to close a lot that is below reserve, just before the gavel is a good time to raise your hand on that lot for the first time. Here is a ringman calling to the auctioneer, "New money!" to rebuild momentum. It is much harder to rebuild momentum than to keep it going.

or lost interest. If the car does bid up more, you are likely competing against the last man to bid (not three or four people). When you emerge the winning bidder, having stuck to your bottom line, the crowd just might thunder in recognition of the victory or at least privately acknowledge your auction acumen. The situation has been maneuvered to your advantage, and you have secured the dream car at the price of your choosing. Now, go get one of those free beers.

Protect Yourself

Know the buyer's rights with the auction house. Read the bidder agreement. In a world inundated with scroll-and-click legal notices, this is not one of those times to click it and forget it.

Some auctions limit any recourse for problems with the purchase to 30 days as part of the bidder agreement. The car may not even be home by then. So, document the car's condition and every item, including documentation, that was included in the sale. Check it again immediately after the sale, make sure the car was not damaged or items have gone missing between the time it was first inspected and the time of signing the winning bidder slip.

Let your insurance company know that you intend to bid on a car. The moment the bid is won, contact them and have them bind coverage. If there are any issues

...is true in martial arts and in auction buying: protect ...ourself at all times. One good way to do that is to employ ... professional inspector to evaluate a potential car. Let the ...spector give valid, objective data to base any affection ...or the car. Perhaps knowing it is a good car before bid-...ling will help you bid prouder than the next guy, needing ... hedge his bid in anticipation of unknown issues.

...r the pace of the bidding and auctioneer call is rapid but ...he owner just won't lift the reserve, then he will quickly ...lose the bid. Good. That will give you an opportunity to ...egotiate a better deal afterward instead of running up ...he bid. Sometimes the best move is not to play.

...ommunicate them to the auction staff immediately. Be ...ertain any issues are addressed before settling with the ...uction house.

Have transportation arrangements made before bid-...ing and make them the next call after the insurance ...ompany. Getting a quote on-site will almost certainly ...ost more, and you have little control over the quality of ...he driver or carrier being offered.

Once transport is arranged, look over the car one last ...ime, take photos of the car, and note any significant

blemishes or flaws. Compare these photos to the driver's pickup inspection report and your personal inspection once the new acquisition arrives at your home. If there are any discrepancies, there is documented proof backed by your insurance company's attorneys, not just your word against the auction house or transport company.

Know When You Just Don't Know

Sometimes the best way to win at the auction game is to simply just not play or at least know when to send in a pinch hitter. As much as this book is about getting the most out of your collection when you sell it, I spend most of the time talking about all that goes into selection and purchase. The reason is very simple: the money is made when a car is bought and collected when it is sold.

An auction house charges 8 percent up to as much 20 percent (when figuring in both seller's and buyer's premiums) for an experience—call it proximity plus entertainment. They also design a great deal of confusion into the process. That is on purpose. Even the bid call is designed to hold attention on them, to avoid bidders seeing the competition, and to control the pace to keep bidders off balance.

An effective auction bid call will keep a bidder hyper-focused and in an emotionally charged state of hypervigilance. The environment is designed to disorient and overload the senses to dull sensemaking abilities. Think of trying to buy a car from an Agent Smith army inside the matrix.

Hiring a broker or a buyer's agent may seem counter-intuitive since paying an additional 5- to 10-percent fee on top of the auction settlement price of a vehicle seems like an added expense. However, hiring someone to buy for you helps you make sense out of a situation and a vehicle, saving time, saving money, and more impor-tantly saving you from making a costly purchase mistake. Having Neo on the inside may prove to be quite handy and end up saving more than all those costs combined. That isn't limited to the auction environment, either. The same can be said when looking for cars within pri-vate collections.

Broker

Most people think of a broker as little more than a spotter or a bird dog. In fact, that is the term used to describe the nominal fee a person is paid for bringing attention to something of value. A professional broker does much more than simply show cars. Even in our ultra-connected social media–driven society, sourcing high-quality cars takes skill. Knowing who has worth-while collections and who is trustworthy takes relation-ships that are sometimes decades in the making.

5 VEHICLE INSPECTION: TRUST BUT VERIFY

Detach yourself emotionally from the purchase. Determine your standards and stay faithful to them, no matter how exciting a car looks at first blush. Knowing your conditions of satisfaction and your purpose of the purchase and sticking to them satisfies the emotion behind the purchase in the first place.

The more you like a car, the tougher it should be scrutinized.

Three Must-Ask Questions and Three Main Areas for Inspection

Instead of rating a car with an oversimplified numbering system, typically 1 to 6, I consider the quality of a car using three metrics: principal use, condition grade, and overall originality. Taken together as a guideline, a quality matrix provides the ability to quickly ascertain what a car is and

The scope and areas of importance of a quality inspection vary widely depending upon the kind of car and how the buyer intends to use it. Don't bother sending a concours judge to evaluate this undercarriage. There is nothing as originally equipped about it. This is just like in the shop or garage; pick the right tool for the right job.

Here is the top side of the same car in the previous picture. This 1970 Dodge Dart Swinger won't be mistaken for a daily driver. The question is, once the car is bought, how do you plan on spending time with it?

what it is not. The matrix is a valuable tool in determining how good of a fit a collectible vehicle is to a prospective purchaser's intended use, personal preferences, and collecting goals.

Principal Use

How is the current owner using the car? Learn how to ask the right questions in the right way. Review the principal uses outlined in the first chapter. Ask good probing questions to find out which category the car lands in:

- Project car
- Daily driver
- Seasonal driver
- Driven show car
- Trailered show car
- Private museum piece
- Public museum piece

Condition

In what condition is the car currently? I outline various factors here: cosmetic condition and mechanical condition. How does the condition (fit and finish) and methods of restoration compare to "as showroom new"?

Condition refers to anything that money and time can fix on a car. Throwing money at a car won't make it more original than it was when it first rolled off the assembly line. No matter how much time is spent restoring a car to like-new fit and finish, provenance cannot be boosted. Condition is the one thing that can't be improved on a collectible car. So, when price is a factor in buying the best car that can be found, it is the one factor with the most flexibility.

There are several areas to consider when grading a car's condition and several variables to consider when buying within each area. This can turn into a rabbit hole deep enough to fill an entirely new book, so here's a quick overview of these specific areas. Within each, two different types are outlined: cosmetic and mechanical condition. How does the operation, fit and finish, state of preservation, or methods of restoration compared to "as showroom new"?

Exterior

When most people think of the exterior condition of the vehicle, they first think "paint and body." They are right—in part. Paint, bodywork, and sheet metal

Facing page: Misinformation can innocently pass from one owner to the next without detection. The same is the case for unsubstantiated rumors about certain cars on the internet. When collecting cars for fun and/or profit, be certain. Here is acknowledged Mopar expert Frank Badalson inspecting a questionable dash VIN plate. The verdict was that it is original but poorly restored sometime during the car's life. Now that it has been verified, it can be trusted.

are all important, but they are not the entire picture. The exterior condition also includes the window glass, marker lights, headlight assemblies, front grille, bumpers, taillight bezels, as well as all badging and graphics.

When it comes to these items, condition is paramount. If they are not operable or condition has degraded to an unacceptable level of appearance, they need to be refurbished or replaced. With every component that is replaced with a reproduction, the less original the vehicle becomes. Even if the car looks perfect, it is still less of the vehicle that rolled off the original assembly line. There is a saying in the hobby that reproduction parts have no collector value. By that logic, an assembly of new reproduction parts may look cool, but it has less collector value than a car in the same condition but comprised of original parts.

So, when evaluating a car for condition, know which exterior trim parts are restorable, which have an ample supply of factory replacement parts, and most importantly which parts are neither reproduced nor can be replaced by a factory-original piece of the same like and kind. Missing trim, light assemblies, or glass could turn a promising upside to the purchase into a money pit that is difficult to complete. The balance to strike is between cosmetic beauty, functionality, and originality of the vehicle's components. The most optimal combination is like-new cosmetics, fully functional, while retaining as much originality as possible.

The same reasoning applies to the paint and body. People like a pretty car; there is no doubt that beauty rings the cash register and raises the pulse rate. Underneath a glowing skin, make sure that the car has solid bones and original sheet metal. Most people who are into cars knows enough to bring a magnet to check for body filler when looking at a car.

There are many signs that can readily be seen when evaluating the quality of bodywork lurking underneath the paint. In my company, the inspectors use a paint blemish key to identify and notate them. The other aspect of rating paint and body condition is overall panel fit and finish. Panels should fit uniformly with even gaps between them. The color and shade of each panel should match. The patina, or general wear, should be the same from panel to panel. Ideally, look for a vehicle that is rust free and retains all of its original sheet metal.

If a car has been restored, it may be more difficult to detect original sheet metal from that which was sourced from a donor body, a factory-original replacement, or an aftermarket reproduction. If any panel replacement or body repair has been done to an undetectable standard, the condition is considered "as good as new."

Just like trim and glass pieces, if a car has inferior repairs, unrepaired damage, or body rot caused by rust, make sure that the proper replacement pieces can be source before committing to purchase. Many makes and models have signature places where the body rusts. Learn what those are for the target vehicle and be sure to check them. If these problem areas include integral structural components, such as a frame rail, firewall, or roof pillar, consider moving on to a healthier candidate.

While condition-grading cars, vehicles with structural collision or rust damage automatically fall into the "parts car" category. As vehicles rise in desirability and rarity, it is vital to know how sound the foundation of the vehicle is because these are also the ones that are most susceptible to be "resurrected" instead of merely restored.

Interior

The easy way most hobbyists use to freshen up the interior of their vintage collectible is with new carpet and a new set of seat skins. That does not make the rest of the interior in like-new condition. The easiest way to ascertain the overall quality of the condition is to compare the patina of those areas within the interior that are less likely to be replaced with those high-touch areas that are easily updated.

The door pull and steering wheel are less likely to be removed and restored than the seat cover of the driver seat on a vehicle that benefitted from a simple refresh. A patina mismatch is a glaring discontinuity that undermines what has been replaced or refurbished. Seeing new material next to old makes the old look even more worn. The overall effect feels like shortcuts were taken with the car. When condition grading an interior, work from the most difficult to replace outward to discern how close to factory new a car is.

Dash

The other area commonly missed when considering the condition of the interior is under the dash. It is also the most popular place to cut corners. Every gauge bezel, knob, and lens can be new, and everything seems to operate as intended, but how does the wire harness look underneath? Look for bad splices, worn and brittle wires, broken connectors, or evidence of excessive moisture. All of this could point to a cosmetic but not mechanical restoration.

It does not matter if the interior has all new skin and trim if all the wiring is 50 years old, representing a fire hazard waiting to happen. As factory new means just that: everything is like new including what can be seen and what cannot.

Engine Bay

The best way to quickly ascertain the condition of a stock engine bay of a vehicle is to be familiar with which normal wear parts are commonly replaced and at what intervals. Cross reference this with the odometer reading and see if they are congruent. If there appears to be more aftermarket or service replacement parts than one would anticipate, then the car has lived a harder life than the odometer indicates.

> "The best way to quickly ascertain the condition of a stock engine bay of a vehicle is to be familiar with which normal wear parts are commonly replaced and at what intervals."

On contemporary classics, look for yellow grease pencil notations as an indication of components being replaced as part of a collision repair or major mechanical failure. Look beyond the grease (or the gleam if the engine has had a good detail) and check casting and date codes of parts to make sure they are correct for the car.

Then, look for signs of mechanical problems. Gas stains on the intake manifold could indicate a fuel system leak. Soot marks around exhaust ports could point to a failed exhaust manifold gasket or a cracked manifold. Oil leaks from the valve covers could mean that the valve cover bolts need to be retorqued or the gaskets need to be replaced. This is just a short list of examples, but the order of operations is the same in all areas.

First, check if the component is original and correct as would be expected to be given the mileage. Second, check if are there any signs of massive component repair or replacement. Third, make sure that everything is operating as intended. Fourth and finally, does it look pretty?

Most people run this list in the opposite direction and stop once they see that the engine bay looks pretty. This results in misgrading the engine bay for condition and is usually a purchase mistake. A buyer may end up with a beautiful-looking engine bay missing thousands of dollars in correct or original parts that are expensive or nearly impossible to source.

Conversely, I would sooner pay more for a car that operates as it should, has all its original engine assembly parts, but factory finishes are failing or covered in a well-earned coat of grime from the miles traveled. I can throw money and time at cosmetics to bring the engine bay back to showroom new but will have a much harder time replacing a date-code-correct component that has been out of production for 30-plus years.

Chassis

This is the place to look the hardest for rust. This is the place most car flippers work hardest to hide rust issues instead of properly addressing them. The resulting trend in restoration is to obliterate the lines between factory installed sound insulation and corrosion resistance with that of aftermarket undercoat used to conceal or encapsulate rust.

Fully restored cars tend to make the undercarriages so nice that owners dread to even drive them, which defeats the purpose of enjoying them. Current restoration and preservation trends value presenting collector cars as they were when they rolled off the assembly line with the undercoat included.

If the car was "born" equipped with undercoating, that is how it should remain or be restored. Many solid cars have been dismissed or undervalued because of the fear of undercoat. This means that a buyer must be better in determining if rusty floorboards and suspension components are slathered in POR15 to hide cancer or if pristine sheet metal and frame rails were treated with a factory undercoating agent.

It would be a mistake to condition grade a car as "poor" simply because it has been treated with undercoating. In addition to comparing the quality of finish on the suspension, fuel system, and brake components to that of new, you should learn what factory undercoat materials and application patterns look like and use those as a baseline for comparison. Most aftermarket undercoat applications designed to encapsulate rust is sloppy and thick and coats the floor pans, suspension components, fuel and brake lines, etc. It is usually easy to tell it apart from a factory installation, and it does severely impact the condition grading of the undercarriage.

Undercoat or no undercoat, factory or otherwise, the best way to tell if there are rust issues that require major surgery is to not only visually check for evidence of rust and rust repair but also check the frame rails, floor pan welds, suspension mounts, and the like for structural integrity. The welds and floor pan seams should be consistent with what the factory produced.

Tubular steel, such as frame rails, can rust from the inside out. This kind of rust scale can be seen through bolt access or drain holes. If any rust scale is visible, test these areas for metal fatigue. They should have the same thickness and strength. If there is any "give" or flimsiness, then the metal has likely been compromised, which

This is a 1974 Plymouth Duster 360 4-speed with 28,000 original miles. It still wears its original paint, interior, and unrestored undercarriage. Outwardly, the only thing not stock about the car is the wheel and tire package. It is only driven sparingly every summer, but certainly not considered a seasonal driver, more like a driven show car. Nothing I just described tells anything about the car's condition. In that department, it rates an overall Very Good to Excellent.

requires repair or replacement. There may be a business case for doing so. Make sure that these parts are available.

If you are committed to repair the problem, doing so to that undetectable standard is the best way to pay yourself back when it comes time to sell. Any obvious patches welded in place or any improvised sheet-metal work diminishes the condition of the vehicle, even if the workmanship is sound.

Overall Driving

Many number-one-condition trailer queens are not in fact in 100-percent factory new for the simple reason that they do not mechanically perform as a brand-new car would. A vehicle's ability to start, run smoothly, drive, maneuver, and stop as the factory intended is as

intrinsic to the condition of the vehicle as is the luster of the paint work. Make sure that everything works and the car is in good tune before condition grading a vehicle or be sure to account for the fact that it is not when evaluating it.

> "A vehicle's ability to start, run smoothly, drive, maneuver, and stop as the factory intended is as intrinsic to the condition of the vehicle as is the luster of the paint work."

Condition Grades

Better than New

Every component and surface is finished to exceed the quality achieved by the factory. Mechanical operation and overall fit and finish exceed that of the original manufacturer. No discernible wear.

Better than New is self-explanatory. The exhaust system, third member, and suspension detail here far exceed anything Chrysler was churning out in 1970.

New

As delivered by the selling dealer complete with a manufacturer's warranty. Not previously titled or used by a private owner. No discernible wear.

New can be just that: the condition a car was in when you first saw it in the showroom, before they handed over the keys. It can also mean restored to that very standard, similar to the front suspension detail on this 1970 Challenger 440 six-pack convertible. It is stone immaculate but still shows overspray, paint runs, and places where the primer still peaks through the topcoat. These conditions are precisely what could be found on a Chrysler product produced in 1970.

Like New

99 to 100 percent of new. Previously titled or used by a private owner. Impeccably kept, this vehicle has no discernible mechanical and/or cosmetic problems and has a clean engine bay and chassis.

This 2014 Shelby GT500 has fewer than 2,500 miles on it. It was never driven in the rain and stored in a climate-controlled garage. It truly is Like New.

Like New Minus

97 to 99 percent of as-delivered condition. Extremely slight wear is only seen upon very close inspection consistent with very limited public showing, climate-controlled storage, seldom driven, and impeccably maintained.

This might seem like splitting hairs, but this 1970 Mercury Cougar convertible is best described as Like New Minus because it shows just a touch more wear than the 2014 Shelby. The fading paper tags on the rear axle, dulling finish on the gas tank, and the oxidation between leaf springs and clamps all bear witness to being carted around the country for a season of car shows and occasional sunny drives. Sitting by itself, most people would consider it a number-one-condition vehicle on the 1 to 6 scale.

Excellent Plus

90 to 96 percent of showroom condition. Exceptionally nice. May have slight wear on exterior and interior finishes but visible only under close inspection consistent with years of show detailing, climate-controlled storage, enclosed transport, and indoor display. Most cars in this class are not driven more than a few miles per year.

This 1970 Ford Mustang Mach 1 was rotisserie restored 20 years ago. Even though it has been well cared for, it is beginning to show wear. This wear and tear are noticeable and not remedied by cleaning or detailing. The primer finish on the floorboards of this vehicle is beginning to fail. Also, notice that the steel brake and fuel lines are beginning to oxidize. The floors of this vehicle as well as other areas need to be refurbished to be considered Like New.

Excellent

80 to 89 percent of new condition. Shows minimal wear. High-touch surfaces have small blemishes and/or flaws and plated finishes have dulled. Components may show patina and/or blemishes consistent with repeated show detailing, transport, occasional driving on dry roads, and outdoor display.

This unrestored, outwardly original 1974 Plymouth Satellite Sebring Restomod still wears 100 percent of its original paint. All areas (exterior, engine bay, interior, and undercarriage) considered, this car rates in Excellent condition. Most of the 11 to 20 percent of wear compared to New can be found on the undercarriage. This is the cleanest a car can be and still be driven on a regular basis.

Very Good
70 to 79 percent of as-delivered condition. All equipment is working as designed. In all areas, the patina is of normal aging and wear but consistent with a well-maintained car, driven on a limited basis, and indoor storage.

By the time a car gets to Very Good, things like this will be noticeable: thin spots in the paint beginning to oxidize. This AMC Javelin will still look good at more than 10 feet away, but walk up on the car and the patina is apparent. Frankly, this condition grade is amazing on a 48-year-old original paint car. It is a sign of a well-cared-for car that was also responsibly driven and enjoyed. If this were the roof of a car built in 2014 and not 1972, that assessment would be completely different.

Fair
55 to 69 percent of showroom-new condition. This car shows more than average wear. The car's major components function, and it runs and drives but may need repairs to minor mechanical systems. Any two main areas (exterior, interior, engine bay, or chassis) may be worn beyond service life, requiring refurbishment or component replacement.

Once you get into Fair territory, a car usually tends to need cosmetic attention in one or more areas. This 1967 Corvette's wheel lip has obviously been in unvoluntary contact with the oversized tires stuffed underneath it. The other side is the same way. All things considered, the car needs body repair in several areas and a complete repaint to improve at all in condition grade.

Project

51 to 65 percent of new condition. May or may not be running, perhaps missing a few factory components but all the major components are present. This car is structurally sound but requires complete mechanical and cosmetic restoration of the exterior, interior, engine bay, and chassis.

This is a tremendous example of a project car that can be driven while parts are gathered and decisions made as to what direction you wish to take it. Because it is a vintage Pontiac LeMans convertible and not its cousin the GTO, it also puts it within the realm of affordability for someone looking to enter the hobby.

Parts Car

Diminished beyond 50 percent of showroom condition. This vehicle is missing many parts and/or has deteriorated to the point of not being a practical restoration candidate.

At first glance, this 1979 Pontiac Trans Am looks like a solid driver. Upon further inspection, the car is rough in every area examined with very little that can be preserved or refurbished. Between the extent of sheet-metal and chassis rust, body damage, and bleached-out interior trim, there was very little left to restore. This is an example of a car that has been neglected to the point that it is no longer even a project car. It's time to start looking for parts to salvage from this beleaguered bird.

Originality

How original is the car? The various different types of originality are seen in this section. How important is original paint and original engine? Are the components "typical" or "not typical" to factory original? How correct is a restored car is compared to how it was when new? How is this all proven?

Originality Categories

Unrestored as Factory Equipped

An unrestored vehicle in near factory condition in more than one or all the following areas: exterior, interior, engine bay, and chassis.

This is a certified benchmark original 1971 Chevrolet Corvette factory equipped with an LS6 454. This is the epitome of Unrestored as Factory Equipped. This car is worth twice what a restored example would fetch.

Restored as Factory Equipped

The vehicle has usually been professionally restored to the current highest standard, using only refurbished original parts and NOS factory parts. Strict adherence is paid to replicating factory fit, finishes, and marking details. All bare metal and plated finishes must be as factory produced. Paint and body must approximate factory fit and finish.

This 1978 Pontiac Trans Am SE began as a 15,619-original-mile example in Excellent condition and then was restored as factory optioned, even using NOS interior cloth material.

Restored Concours

The vehicle has usually been professionally restored to the current highest standard using a combination of refurbished original parts, exact reproduction parts, and NOS parts. Attention is paid to replicating factory fit, finishes, and marking details. Bare metal finishes may be mimicked with paints and coatings to prevent corrosion. Paint and body may exceed the quality produced by the factory.

This OEM Gold Certified 1969 Dodge Daytona is a prime example of Restored as Factory Equipped. There are no reproduction parts used on this car right down to the plug wires and fuel filter. As restoration fads come and go, even in the Restored Concours category, this car will remain a consistent benchmark for what a Daytona looked like in 1969.

Pure Stock Appearing

A restored car in near factory condition where the equipment of the vehicle match the VIN and documentation description. This type of restoration may incorporate many aftermarket reproduction parts. The car will appear stock in a broad sense, the fine factory details are not adhered to.

This 1966 Corvette roadster is a solid example of a Pure Stock Appearing vehicle. There is a fair number of reproduction parts on the car. Factory fit, finish, and markings are not slavishly adhered to. Even one hideaway headlight housing is an original metal unit, the other a fiberglass reproduction. This is a driver-quality restoration.

Personalized Stock

A largely stock-appearing car, restored or unrestored, that is near factory condition with three or more exceptions, including exterior or interior color change or bolt-on parts such as aftermarket tires, radio, ignition, or exhaust.

This GTO convertible is a good example of Personalized Stock. It retains an original drivetrain, although it is upfitted with an OEM-style Tri-Power carburetor/intake setup, period-appropriate but non-factory Hurst Wheels, and a modern stereo system. It is tastefully updated from factory but not restyled.

Restomod

A mostly outwardly stock-appearing car, usually restored with drivetrain and performance components upgrades with bolt-on performance-enhancing parts. Could extend to a full drivetrain and suspension swap working within the constraints of the stock frame and sheet metal. These modifications are largely reversible without cutting or welding.

This 1967 Corvette roadster takes things to the next level into full Restomod with a modern wheel and tire package, modern LS engine, and upgraded suspension using factory frame and hard points. The brakes are also state-of-the art. The interior is largely stock appearing but rendered in upgraded materials like glove leather and precision digital/analog gauges.

Highly Modified

Outward appearance is modified, including paint and external sheet metal to accentuate the factory stock lines. Interior, chassis, and drivetrain are likewise modified to fit the personal tastes of the owner without constraint of the factory fixtures, stock sheet metal, or trim. Still readily recognizable as a given make and model. These modifications are not easy or practical to reverse.

You can see right away that this 1971 Plymouth Road Runner is Highly Modified. The front clip was hand fabricated all in metal, complete with hideaway headlights. The back of the car was modified to accept a functional rear wing. The result is a one-of-none 1971 Plymouth Superbird.

Full Custom

Vehicle modified to fulfill the vision of the owner and its builder. Custom fabrication is evident in every area of the vehicle, sometimes obscuring the identity of the original donor vehicle.

This 1929 Ford Model A is far from stock. Yet, you can still tell what it was originally. Every line has been tweaked a bit. The metal work was all left raw so you can see every seam. The frame was certainly not original to the car. In the interior, not one original factory component remains. The same goes for the engine bay. The Ford Model A has been a popular platform for customizing for nearly 100 years. It will be interesting to see what takes over in the next generation.

When to Call the Experts: Third-Party Inspectors

Retaining a professional inspector can be a matter of convenience, saving a buyer from a long drive or an airline flight to test drive a car or confirm condition. That is a valid reason to hire out a prepurchase inspection, but this type of inspection doesn't require a set of eyeballs that are expert in a specific car. If you can take the time and generally know your way around a vehicle, it is best to go see the car yourself.

You may find that the car doesn't strike your fancy the way it did in photos. Sit in it. Drive it yourself if you plan on driving it a lot because your personal comfort counts. A third-party inspector can't do that for you.

If you are buying a car principally based on its authenticity or overall originality, even if you can make the trip, hire a quality marque expert to survey the car. The expert can make sure that everything is original, correct, and most importantly all the VIN stamps and casting codes are correct and original to the car.

Earlier I wrote about being aware of conflicts of interest when hiring a third-party vendor. Even if the vendor does not have any apparent interest that it will put ahead of the buyer, still be aware of bias when retaining an inspector. Automobile enthusiasts tend to be an opinionated lot.

An inspector who is also a concours judge or operates a restoration shop by day will take his or her baseline assumptions into the inspection field. Every inspector has an idea of how a car should be, not considering how the car was represented to the buyer or what the buyer's intended use for the car is. That is generally good, but it can also result in receiving bad data.

> "Every inspector has an idea of how a car should be, not considering how the car was represented to the buyer or what the buyer's intended use for the car is."

It is more important for some makes and models than others to have independent third-party verification of the drivetrain VINs and casting codes to ensure the authenticity of the vehicle. This 1969 Chevrolet Chevelle SS L78 in special-order Rally Green is light on paperwork but confirmed 100-percent authentic thanks to the detailed inspection and catalog of every component of the vehicle by an acknowledged subject-matter expert.

The best way to identify the right inspector for the job is to match your intended use with their areas of strength or core competency. For a car that was represented as concours award winning, hire a concours judge familiar with the judging standard that was applied to the car when it won. That same inspector may be the wrong fit for looking at a Restomod summer driver. The report will likely come back riddled with red ink about what components are incorrect, a laundry list of incorrect finished and missing factory inspection marks, and then an accounting of the high cost to bring the car back to showroom-new OEM specifications. It would be enough to scare anyone away.

If you are looking at a hot rod or a Full Custom street car, find a person who builds them for a living and have that person inspect the car. Ask that person to look at the general engineering and workmanship and to ignore some of the styling choices. He or she may reveal his or her own bias by sharing what design choices the person would have made or what other parts he or she would have chosen. If you find the car appealing, that person just needs to say if the car is mechanically sound and that the workmanship of the build is solid, not their opinion of personal tastes.

When to Put in an Offer and When to Pull the Plug

If the car checks out completely as described and is as good as or in superior condition than represented, pay the agreed price and complete the deal. It doesn't happen that way very often.

Think of it as if it was a final inspection for a new home. There are always a few things that the owner failed to mention or the buyer failed to notice or ask about. That is what a prepurchase inspection is for.

Typically, inspectors find that some deferred maintenance, stale gas, and dead batteries are almost the rule rather than the exception. For small items such as these, negotiate a fix that the seller will complete before finalizing the sale, or arrange for a credit against the agreed sales price and remedy the items yourself. Either way, if the car is largely as anticipated, go ahead and buy it.

Buyers can also avoid opening a can of worms. If there are signs of shortcuts taken during a restoration, evidence of rust or collision repair that was not previously disclosed, or perhaps the car just has a simplex of mechanical issues that need immediate attention, cut bait and cancel the deal.

Now, if angling for a project car, then maybe these are items that can be leveraged to the buyer's advantage

Another form of expert inspection comes into play when none of the numbers match. To judge the quality of fabricated work, hire a master fabricator to evaluate it. Just make sure not to ask someone to grade their own work. See the radiator hose disappearing into the frame on this 1929 Ford hot rod? That's because the frame is also the coolant tank. It doesn't get much cooler than that.

when negotiating. The objective is to detect and eliminate any question marks the car has *before* it is legally owned.

Failing to be willing, ready, and able to walk away has caused heartburn for a great many auto enthusiasts over the years. You would not be the first to buy a car and then perform a complete drivetrain and suspension rebuild. But being willing to walk away (even when this close) makes a buyer happier in the long run rather than taking on someone else's headache.

If there are questions of authenticity that cannot be answered or a possibility that the paperwork or VIN stamps, trim tags, etc. are inauthentic, cancel the deal. Do not be the one trying to overcome the idea that this is correct and original even though it has a re-stamped motor, fake fender tag, or made-up build sheet. Pull the plug. Walk away. This is supposed to be about your dream car, not a monster in your garage.

Here is an ounce of prevention waiting to happen. The outside bolster of the driver's seat is a common wear spot even on the lowest of mileage 1996 Viper GTSs. This car has logged only 9,000 miles on the odometer, but there it is. Rather than a small tear impeaching the entire car, have it fixed. You will take away a negotiation point when haggling over the price with the potential buyer, one that would likely cost two to three times the repair itself.

WHAT TO DO AFTER PURCHASING A VEHICLE

It used to be unimaginable to buy even a paperback book over the internet. Now, it is often difficult to find a bookstore in most neighborhoods. These days we do the same for furniture, shoes, pants, and even underwear. That said, I have been facilitating long-distance purchases of investment-quality vehicles for about 20 years—long before people were comfortable buying their unmentionables online.

Based on my experience completing thousands of transactions in all 50 states, most every Canadian province, and more than 46 foreign countries, I can say two things: First, buying a collector car is more personal than picking out that next package of tighty-whities. Second, it does not matter if the car is bought off a dealer's showroom, the auction tent, or an online listing. There is little time and a long to-do list to ensure that the car arrives complete and exactly as expected.

Car buying, especially vintage car buying, has still been largely an in-person affair. In this traditional way, an inquiry is made, many questions are asked, and a time is

Here is what many consider the king of full-sized fun during the muscle car era: a 1969 Chevrolet Impala SS 427 4-speed. Garnet Red with white interior, Unrestored as Factory Equipped, and in Excellent condition. Now that you've negotiated a price and placed a deposit to hold the car while you complete your homework, the real work begins.

Engine/Transmission Evaluation (section 5)

5a. What type of engine does it have? *Matching 383*

5b. Has the engine been rebuilt? Yes ☒ No ☐   By Whom? Phone Date of Rebuild: *2018 Automotive Machine Fraser, MI.*

5c. Is the engine oil clean? Yes ☒ No ☐   Dark or black colored oil indicates a change is necessary and may be indicative of past maintenance trends.

5d. When was the last oil change? *New* Overdue? Yes ☐ No ☒

5e. Check for a leaking oil pan gasket. Pass ☒ Fail ☐

5f. Check for a leaking front/rear main seal. Pass ☒ Fail ☐

5g. What type of transmission does it have? *Matching 727*   Supporting Documentation: *Vin on side*

5h. Has the transmission been rebuilt? Yes ☒ No ☐   By Whom? Phone Date of Rebuild: *Winners auto + cycle Brownstown MI.*

5i. If equipped with standard transmission, has the clutch ever been replaced? Yes ☐ No ☐   When? Where? What mileage?

N/A

5j. Check the master cylinder and slave cylinder for leakage. Pass ☒ Fail ☐

5k. Is the transmission fluid clean? Yes ☒ No ☐   Dark or brown colored fluid indicates a change is necessary and may be indicative transmission damage or poor maintenance habits.

5L. When was the last transmission change? _____ Overdue? Yes ☐ No ☐ *During resto rebuild*

5m. Check for a leaking transmission pan gasket. Pass ☒ Fail ☐

5n. Check all coolant lines for leakage. Pass ☒ Fail ☐

5o. Check the coolant in the reservoir. A brown frothy mixture in the reservoir usually indicates oil and water mixing in the oil filter/cooler housing. Pass ☐ Fail ☐   *N/A*

5p. Inspect the fuel lines going to the fuel rail for brittleness or cracking. Pass ☒ Fail ☐

5q. Inspect the plug wires for brittleness or cracking. Pass ☒ Fail ☐

5r. Inspect the brake fluid for color. Black colored brake fluid indicates a change is necessary. Pass ☒ Fail ☐

5s. Is the air filter clean? Pass ☒ Fail ☐

5t. Is the engine bay clean and neat? All hoses / wiring in correct place? Pass ☒ Fail ☐ *DETAILED!*

5u. Is the battery in good condition? Yes ☒ No ☐

Engine/Transmission Condition Notes (comment on anything checked "No"):

EXCELLENT.

Stick to the checklist to make sure you will be as happy with the car when it is your own garage as you were when it was sitting under the auction lights.

scheduled to see the car in person. Once you've seen it, shake the seller's hand and pay him or her. It sounds simple. This may still work when buying a collector car locally. The "after" part of the sale is short, spanning the time it takes to trade dollars for title, turn the key, and drive off. It is also easy to overlook many details in the excitement of that moment.

With collectible cars costing tens of thousands of dollars and often located far away, this tried-and-true workflow of automobile purchase just doesn't work as well. Most often, buying involves long road trips or plane flights only to find the buyer's definition of "excellent" is far from the seller's opinion.

The other pitfall to the traditional buying cycle is

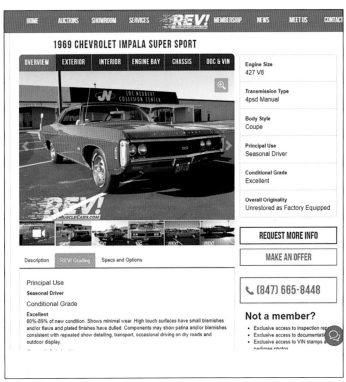

Carefully review how the car was represented again. This ad claims that the car is a factory-original L72 427/425-hp SS, it is rust free, and it retains its 100-percent numbers-matching original drivetrain. Before completing the transaction, be certain to verify these points.

Here is the owner's representation of the vehicle as presented, which confirms what I already knew about the car from previous experience. This is a benchmark-quality Unrestored as Factory Equipped car in Excellent Plus condition and has been principally used as a private museum piece for the last couple decades and a driven show car before that.

osing out on good cars because someone else scoops it up while you are still lining up a personal visit or hiring a professional inspector. Buyers must balance diligence with flexibility and speed to secure the purchase before someone else does.

Some people can afford to be aggressive and maybe even a little reckless to make sure they get the first crack at buying a collectible car. The strategy here is to optimize both, pursuing a car in a "quick but careful" fashion. This means being aggressive about both closing a sale with the seller and verifying that the purchase includes everything it is supposed to and is also precisely as described.

No matter where the car is purchased, make sure that the new investment is protected. These steps to make

certain the car is correct and completely as represented varies from venue to venue. When buying from a private party, whether that be directly or through a professional intermediary, set the ground rules and timeline to do your due diligence, confirm condition, and make sure all the documentation, spares, and anything else related to the vehicle is accounted for.

With a dealer, often buyers have only the hour or so spent looking at the car in the showroom. The moment the deal is struck and the cash is paid, the "as is, where is" sale is complete. Buyers are completely on the hook for any hidden deficiency or omissions missed during the showing.

When buying a car at auction, read the bidder's contract. Buyers may have as little as 10 days or as much as a month to address and receive any remedy for any issue that comes to light. When a buyer is excited about a new car, it is easy to lose sight of the details. So, protect that enthusiasm by remaining focused on the details.

There are five tools a buyer can use to make sure they secure the sale and are certain that what is expected ends up in their driveway. These tools may seem familiar: deposit, bill of sale or purchase agreement, inspection, final payment, and transportation.

Using the Purchase Agreement to Direct a Private Sale

The agreed sale price is the obvious element of the transaction, but it isn't the only part. Typically, a bill of sale is used mainly as proof of purchase and to let the local department of motor vehicles (DMV) know how much tax it can charge the buyer. The bill of sale, or purchase agreement, is much more than that. It outlines all the other terms of the sale, including any contingencies, such as an inspection prior to finalizing the sale, timing, the method of deposit and final payment, as well as any documentation and parts that are included in the sale.

The purchase agreement is also where a buyer can turn an "as is" sale into some insurance of what they are getting. Whatever the advertisement claims about the vehicle regarding mechanical fitness, cosmetic condition, authenticity, and originality should be outlined in the purchase agreement opening with the phrase "seller warrants." Any agreements made with the seller regarding storage, insurance, and the timing of transport and pickup should also be spelled out in this document.

Even if the car is within driving distance and the plan is to inspect the vehicle yourself prior to completing the deal, once a deal is struck or a price is agreed on, do not hesitate to solidify the sale with a deposit. As part of the price negotiations, include sales terms for making a refundable earnest money deposit to hold the car so that it isn't sold out from under you while you do your due diligence.

> "Even if the car is within driving distance and the plan is to inspect the vehicle yourself prior to completing the deal, once a deal is struck or a price is agreed on, do not hesitate to solidify the sale with a deposit."

Now that the pressure is off, switch from aggressively pursuing the car to aggressively conducting your due diligence. It doesn't have to be a large deposit. Use a mediated service such as PayPal for some consumer protection if the car isn't represented correctly.

Set an appointment to see the car in person. Once the seller has accepted the deposit, write up the purchase agreement to recap the timeline to complete the deal

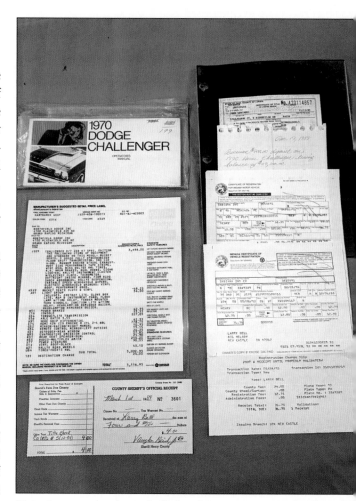

Here is a group shot of all the documentation displayed in an ad. Make sure that the terms of sale on the purchase agreement include these documents. If anything is missing, make sure they are located before settling up. If possible, pay for and bring these documents home instead of risking them being mailed to you. If it is not possible to take personal possession of the documentation at the time of inspection or the deal is being completed remotely, make sure they travel in a sealed envelope inside the car. It is much harder for a transport to lose an entire car and its contents than it is for a shipper to lose an envelope. Every time they move, they are at risk of being lost or damaged.

and the remainder of the terms. Be sure to express in the agreement that the deposit is refundable should the car fail inspection or that any of the documentation or spares are missing. This places the pressure on the seller to make sure everything is present and accounted for before completing the deal. This is important and can save time and trouble in the future tracking down the seller or former owners after the sale in an attempt to address errors or omissions in representation or recover missing items. This is where a purchase verification inspection becomes key.

Purchase Verification

Before getting to the point of finalizing the transaction and picking up the car, a buyer must have a purchase verification inspection to confirm that the car is as represented and still in the same condition as it was advertised in. We have already drilled down in the previous chapter the elements of what makes a good prepurchase inspection. The elements are the same. This is about when to effectively use that tool to meet the objective of protecting the buyer in the purchase without being vulnerable to outside buying competition.

A purchase verification is different than a prepurchase inspection and more like the process of a real estate transaction's final inspection prior to closing. This way, a buyer is less likely to commit an error in his or her haste to secure the car.

A prepurchase inspection is performed before a firm offer is made and with no earnest money paid to secure the car while you check the car. A buyer may be prone to miss details or discount the cost of problems discovered if they are still afraid they may lose out on the opportunity. It is possible to have a prepurchase inspection performed instead of a purchase verification, but there is a risk of losing the car to someone able to move faster or of not being able to come to terms once the inspection is complete.

Putting price negotiations at the front of the deal shows the seller that a buyer is serious and positions the buyer in a place of strength on the back end if the inspection yields any negative surprises. At that point, it is the seller who is afraid of losing the deal, not the buyer.

Final Payment

Upon satisfactory inspection and when any remaining price adjustments have been finalized, it is time for final payment. When completing the sale in person, then the final payment is straightforward. Make sure the title is free and clear of any liens and is signed and dated correctly by the party whose name appears on the front of it. Check the VIN on the title against the VIN on the vehicle itself. Then trade cash or a certified cashier's check for the title and vehicle.

In the event of a long-distance purchase, take the same steps reviewing the title with photos and instruct the seller to overnight ship it with a tracking number. Once the seller has prepared the envelope and has a tracking number on hand, bank wire the proceeds to the seller's account according to their instructions. Be sure to note the year, make, model, and VIN on the outgoing wire notes section.

When doing a post-purchase inspection, be certain to photograph or take a video of the car. Document any pre-existing conditions as well as any areas (top to bottom, high and low) that are susceptible to damage. If it isn't on film, it didn't happen.

Provide the seller with a copy of the wire verification. The title and wire should appear to each side of the transaction no later than the following day. Ideally, transport should pick up the vehicle the same day as the wire hits the seller's account.

Insure the vehicle immediately after purchase. Now that the due diligence has been done, that protects the buyer from 2 tons of disappointment sitting in their driveway and protects it from the time it was paid for to the time it arrives. The moment a purchase agreement is signed and a deposit is placed on the car, call your insurance agent and have a temporary binder of insurance placed on the vehicle. This protects from any loss or liability for the vehicle between the buyer, the seller, and the transport company or any other outside vendor hired to interact with the vehicle.

If something happens to the car before it is safely parked in the buyer's garage, the insurance agency's army of lawyers can contend with the transport company's insurance agency or that of the previous owner. Trying to recover a loss without an insurance company's protection from the date of purchase on the contract is difficult. Protecting yourself from a claim made against you from either party would be even harder.

Third-Party Transport

If a buyer retains a third-party transport company to move the car, there are a few things he or she needs to do. First, confirm that the driver is bonded and insured and that those items are current. If working with a

Date of Inspection: _8/12/19_   Vehicle Inspected at (city, state): _FLAT ROCK MI._

Car Year: _70_ Make: _PLYM._ Model: _road runner_ VIN: _RM27NOG244467_ Body Style: _CONV._

Factory Paint Code: _EF8_   Factory Exterior Trim Code: _____

On _8/12_, I personally inspected and evaluated the vehicle described below for the purpose of providing an objective description of the vehicle's paint, body condition and factory correctness. I inspected this vehicle's exterior paint, frame, bodywork, panel fit, trim, glass, and trunk compartment. This is not an appraisal of the car's value, nor is it a verification or authentication of originality. The observations made in this report are for informational and educational purposes only and shall not in any manner be considered a recommendation or endorsement of any strategy or investment.

Code Inspection Key:

OEPa – Original Equipment Panel	LRPa – Licensed Restoration Panel	ARPa – Aftermarket Replacement Panel	PRPa – Partial Repair Panel	IPPa – Improvised Patch Panel
B - Bent	Ch - Checking	FL – Flaking Paint or Clear Coat	PoC – Painted over Chip(s)	SM – Swirl Marks
Br - Broken	Cr - Cracked	G - Gouged	R - Rubbed	ST - Stained
BB – Buffing Burn	D - Dented	L - Loose	RP – Rivet Pop	T - Torn
BL - Blending	Di - Ding	M - Missing	RU - Rust	TL – Tape Line
Bu - Bubbled	F - Faded	O – Orange Peel	S - Scratched	TP – Thin Paint
BW – Buffing/Wax Residue	Fc – Filled Chip	P - Pitted	SCr – Seam Crack	PR – Paint Run
C - Cut	Fi – Fish Eye	Pc – Paint Chip	SL - Soiled	I - Inclusion

Line Key	Item Description	Inspection Code(s)	Comments
1	**Panel/Trim Condition**	(see key)	**Description of flaw(s)**
1a	Hood		
1b	Front Grill		NO ISSUES
1c	Front Bumper/Trim		
1d	Front Lights		
1e	R Front Fender		
1f	R Front Fender Trim/Lights		FRESH RESTORATION
1g	R Door(s)		
1h	R Door Trim/Glass		
1i	R Side Roof		
1j	R Quarter Panel		EXCELLENT
1k	Trunk Lid		
1l	Rear Bumper/Trim		
1m	Rear Lights		
1n	L Quarter Panel		
1o	L Door(s)		
1p	L Front Fender		

Here is an example of the paint inspection worksheets we use anytime we conduct a paint and body inspection. Notice the extensive key of possible paint conditions. This car, a fresh restoration, shows no significant paint flaws or body issues. Documenting this after purchasing a car and before it is delivered makes it harder for that party who damaged it to avoid liability.

transport broker, make sure this is part of the broker's routine when he or she hires independent operators to transport a vehicle.

Next, the driver will perform a paint inspection upon pickup, noting any blemishes or defects on the bill of lading. Ask them to send a photo of that inspection before they load the car. Compare that inspection to the prepur-

chase or purchase verification inspection to make sure there isn't any new damage between the time the car was inspected and the time that the car was picked up. The same goes for drop-off.

The driver will ask the buyer to sign off on that bill of lading, with those defects noted. Most people, excited to receive their car, quickly sign it and grab the keys

Line Key	Item Description	Inspection Code(s)	Comments
2	**Overall Paint/Body Condition**	Y/N, NA	**Description of flaw(s)**
2a	Does the color match the trim tag color code?	Y	
2b	Does the exterior molding, stripes, and top treatments match the trim tag trim code?	Y	ADDED DUST TRAIL
2c	Has the car ever been repainted? (if so, list why, by whom, how long ago, and what % if known)	Y	PAINTED 2018 DONNY WESTLAND, MI.
2d	Is there evidence of body damage? (list particular evidence including presence of body filler)	N	
2e	Does paint shade on body panels match each other?	Y	
2f	Are there any missing badges, or moldings?	N	
2g	Is the hood aligned evenly side to side, fitting flush?	Y	
2h	Looking down the passenger side from the front to back, are the body panels aligned evenly?	Y	
2i	Looking down the driver side from the front to back, are the body panels aligned evenly?	Y	
2j	Are windshield and backlight trim moldings intact, fitting flush and uniformly?	Y	
2k	Do the doors and trunk lock/unlock correctly with key?	Y	
2l	Is the trunk aligned evenly side to side, fitting flush?	Y	
2m	What kind of finish is used on the frame and floor pans?		FACTORY UNDER COAT REPAINTED
2n	Is there evidence of frame damage or repair?	N	
2o	Is there evidence of rust repair or floor pan replacement?	N	

instead, ask them to point out each one. While they are doing that, make note of any defects that are not on the sheet. Those present and not noted are the responsibility of the shipping company. The same holds true for any mechanical difficulty it reports.

If the prepurchase inspection states the battery checked out okay and the car started without hesitation but the driver reports otherwise, it is possible that the battery was drained or the plugs became fouled by repeated cold starts as they shuffled the car on and off the trailer along their route. There is much more to picking a good transporter than this, but these are the necessary minimums to protect yourself and your car.

Design the Deal to Make the Dealer Work for You

When purchasing a car from a classic or collector car dealership, the sale should flow as close as possible to how it is laid out for dealing with a private party. The difference is knowing where this workflow compliments or conflicts with the dealership's own systems and

Mechanical issues are common with cars that have been sitting in the seller's garage for a while. They are often cold started and not allowed to warm up and blow all the contaminants out of the combustion chamber. The result is a multitude of problems. Whenever possible, start the car. Let it warm up, throttle the gas pedal, make sure the alternator is working, and give the car time to charge the battery. This gives the car at least a small break from the torture of being moved from place to place without ever blowing the cobwebs out of the system before the final move to the buyer's house.

regulatory mandates. One of those mandates is maintaining the privacy of any current or previous owners.

With a collector car, ownership history and paperwork related to the car adds significant value to the car. Do not complete a deal or accept delivery of the car unless all available documentation and historical paperwork related to the vehicle is received.

Dealerships and Documentation

When it comes to documentation, ask to see the originals of all the documentation that the car was advertised with. Most advertisements list a build sheet or broadcast sheet if the car has one. Be sure to ask for other specific factory documents even if they aren't mentioned. The salesperson may not think they are important or may ven have overlooked some items important to the history of the vehicle. From there, create an informal checklist to make sure everything is in your hands.

When it comes to safely shipping documents, it is preferred that items that can be replaced, such as the current title, are shipped overnight with a tracking number. Original factory and historical documents travel safest with the car itself for the simple reason that it is easier or a parcel to become lost or damaged than it is for the entire car to go missing in transport.

Inspection at a Dealership

Buyers can likely hold a car with a deposit and make an offer contingent upon a satisfactory inspection. A first-time collector car buyer should hire a third-party professional who knows what to look for in a dealer-sold car. Be up front with the dealer about your intention to have the car professionally inspected. Arrange, if possible, to have the car hoisted on a lift so the inspector can do a thorough job.

If the inspection misses anything, the dealer will likely shift the responsibility back on the buyer with a brush-off phrase similar to: "What do you expect from a 40-year-old used car?" Avoid that scenario.

There are many issues dealerships can hide but not remedy, including cosmetic deficiencies, mechanical issues, etc. Should the inspector detect them, these items can be powerful leverage in negotiating a credit for anything that is discovered. Depending upon the dealership's capabilities, it may be more advantageous to reduce the price of the vehicle rather than have the dealership address the issue. If it was capable or inclined to do it correctly, it would have been done prior to inspection.

Purchase Agreement at Dealership

Terms of sale language is especially important when buying from professionals. They are experts at insulating themselves from accountability while giving the buyer the appearance of being accommodating. When outlining the terms of the sale, including the deposit, be plain. Buyer satisfaction is the condition of a refundable deposit. If the buyer isn't happy, he or she gets the deposit back. Get that in writing from the dealership as a condition of the sale.

If possible, put a nominal deposit on a credit card to hold the car, buying time to conduct objective due diligence on the vehicle. If you aren't happy and they refuse to refund the deposit, the credit card company is in your corner for any dispute.

Remember to itemize all the paperwork and spare parts that are included with the vehicle in the sale along

This bidder and his boys look at this 1968 Mustang GT 428 Cobra Jet for the first time as the bid dies—the price still seems low. It is desirably equipped but is an older restoration with some broken parts and other parts missing. Let's hope that this bidder keeps his hands in his pockets. The other bidders who did their homework on this car already registered a dollar vote.

with any claims the dealership made when representing the car. Once the deal is complete, if these declarations are not outlined in the bill of sale, the buyer has very little recourse and will have a harder time proving the legal definition of "material misrepresentation."

A well-written terms of sale document keeps dealerships accountable to their word. It also gives both parties a clear outline of what satisfaction means to the buyer and is a valuable tool for good dealers to hold themselves accountable in achieving that.

Auction Pitfalls Part II

I already dedicated a large portion of this book to the auction environment, but some things bear repeating. Remember to keep the buying plan in mind and stay focused on that plan. It is tempting when something looks downright sexy in the auction venue, or worse, it rolls across the block. Those are invitations to failure. Let someone else step into that trap and continue working your plan.

Your homework is preparation for success. Prepare well and success comes as a matter of course. If homework hasn't been done on an eye-catching car, you are now gambling with your success. More to the point, you are flirting with failure.

It's hard to be cautious when you are excited, especially as a neophyte to the auction game. It can even be difficult for seasoned bidders. So, I asked experienced collector Tim Wellborn of the Wellborn Musclecar Museum what rules he follows to keep from being caught up on the ether and come home with an aching in the wallet and a mistake in the garage.

> ## "It's hard to be cautious when you are excited, especially as a neophyte to the auction game. It can even be difficult for seasoned bidders."

Tim Wellborn's Three Simple Rules

I have helped Tim Wellborn bring cars through auction twice, the first time in 2014 and again a few years later. He is also a frequent contributor as a guest Mopar analyst for Mecum on NBC Sports. There is no way would consider Wellborn to be an auction critic. Tha said, even he has three hard and fast rules for avoidin costly purchase mistakes when buying at auction. Thes are guidelines to live by for a first-time buyer seeking th perfect starter vehicle or a seasoned professional addin to an exclusive collection. Follow them to end up with top-shelf car no matter the price point.

1. *Only buy cars you are personally acquainted with.* Thi is self-explanatory. Be familiar with the car's history know what has been done to it over the years, an know the current owner. Then, it is possible to mak an informed purchase decision and avoid any nast surprises.

2. *Only buy cars that are completely unrestored and origina and are verified as such.* This still takes some skill an expertise. It is easier if you have been around the tar

Three simple rules make sure a buyer always comes home with a quality car. This 1966 Plymouth Hemi Satellite pretty much personified these principles.

You may know cars, but a vehicle that has been in a private collection for a number of years is a different beast. You have no idea how well it was kept or what has changed on the vehicle. Even if you think you are familiar, still have the car inspected to verify. With this one, I received a call several months after the sale from a man offering to sell me the original mufflers that came off the car. For a benchmark quality original, those are important, and it was a critical miss on my part during field inspection. Lucky for me, we secured the car for far less than the original auction estimate.

Here is the 1966 Plymouth Hemi Satellite again, now in the staging lanes. This was an exciting purchase, clinching the winning bid just as I described in Chapter 4. Getting it home was uneventful, and all the paperwork outlined on the catalog description arrived intact and accounted for without any drama. I wish I could say they all go down this way.

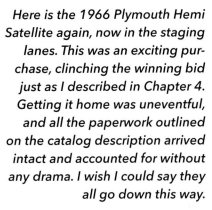

Does this look like a magazine-featured NCRS Top Flight winning car to you? Sadly, this wasn't the condition it was in when we bought it, but this is how the auction house treated it once it changed hands. In stark contrast to the 1966 Hemi purchase, getting this car home was nothing but drama.

get make and model your entire life and know what they were like when they were new. Any car making a "survivor" claim should be scrutinized, if not by yourself then by a trusted independent third party.

3. *Only buy restored cars when you know they've been done by a restorer with a good reputation.* There are finely restored cars. There are fine cars that have been restored. Then, there are resurrections built for the auction block. To the average auction buyer, it is nearly impossible to tell the difference. So, the best way to tell if a restored car headed for the chutes is a good one is to know the reputation of the restorer. Know his or her work habits, the quality of the craftmanship, the person's integrity of character, and his or her standing in the community. Better, have a relationship with that restoration professional and ask that person about the details of the particular car.

If you don't know any of this information, you haven't done your homework and simply don't know what you are bidding on, nor do you have the time to accurately assess it. Is there any other area of your life where you spend significant amounts of money on things you

don't understand? I didn't think so. No amount of TV glitz and momentary excitement should change that.

These are rules for safely buying cars from auctions. The only way to be certain that a car is authentic and not a restored wreck is to buy an unrestored original. This is scalable; unrestored original 1980s, 1990s, or early 2000s cars can just as easily be purchased as high-end vintage muscle. The fact is that auction houses aren't the best places to buy that first collectible car.

Know the House Rules

Make sure to understand the auction house's policies and terms on purchase warranty and conflict resolution, before bidding. In short, read the bidder's contract. Usually, the window of remedy is very short for any issue that the auction house may be responsible for. The buyer may be end up out of pocket for any problems, even if the auction house is at fault, especially if you are just an average Joe without the leverage that comes with being a high-volume consignor or high-rolling buyer.

Here is an illustration: a few years ago, I purchased a 1966 Chevrolet Corvette 427 coupe from one of those glitzy, televised auctions. The car was a recent restoration

Scope of Paint Inspection:

On _1/2/18_ I personally inspected and evaluated the vehicle described below for the purpose of providing an objective description of the vehicle's paint, body condition and factory correctness. I inspected this vehicle's exterior paint, frame, bodywork, panel fit, trim, glass, and trunk compartment. This is not an appraisal of the cars value, nor is it a verification or authentication of originality. The observations made in this report are for informational and educational purposes only and shall not in any manner be considered a recommendation or endorsement of any strategy or investment.

Chev Corvette

Vehicle Inspected at (city, state): _____   Make: _____   Model: _____   Body Style: _____

Year: _66_   VIN: _____   Factory Paint Code: _____   Factory Exterior Trim Code : _____

Code Inspection Key:

OEPa – Original Equipment Panel	LRPa – Licensed Restoration Panel	ARPa – Aftermarket Replacement Panel	PRPa – Partial Repair Panel	IPPa – Improvised Patch Panel
B - Bent	Ch - Checking	FL – Flaking Paint or Clear Coat	PoC – Painted over Chip(s)	SM – Swirl Marks
Br - Broken	Cr - Cracked	G - Gouged	R - Rubbed	ST - Stained
BB – Buffing Burn	D - Dented	L - Loose	RP – Rivet Pop	T - Torn
BL - Blending	Di - Ding	M - Missing	RU - Rust	TL – Tape Line
Bu – Bubbled	F - Faded	O – Orange Peel	S - Scratched	TP – Thin Paint
BW – Buffing/Wax Residue	Fc – Filled Chip	P - Pitted	SCr – Seam Crack	PR – Paint Run
C - Cut	Fi – Fish Eye	Pc – Paint Chip	SL – Soiled	I – Inclusion

Line Key	Item Description	Inspection Code(s) (see key)	Comments
1	**Panel/Trim Condition**		**Description of flaw(s)**
1a	Hood	BW	
1b	Front Grill		
1c	Front Bumper/Trim		
1d	Front Lights		
1e	R Front Fender		
1f	R Front Fender Trim/Lights		
1g	R Door(s)		
1h	R Door Trim/Glass		
1i	R Side Roof	W	
1j	R Quarter Panel		
1k	Trunk Lid		
1l	Rear Bumper/Trim	O	
1m	Rear Lights		
1n	L Quarter Panel		
1o	L Door(s)		
1p	L Front Fender		

Line Key	Item Description	Inspection Code(s)	Comments
2	**Overall Paint/Body Condition**	Y/N, NA	**Description of flaw(s)**
2a	Does the color match the trim	Y	

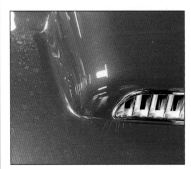

Here is the paint and body inspection for the 1966 Corvette by the transport company picking up the car. It was the definition of flawless when it rolled across the auction block, but that isn't what left the auction grounds.

complete with National Corvette Restorers Society (NCRS) judging sheets and fresh off a recent magazine feature photoshoot. If there was ever a car that approached perfection, it was this.

As a matter of course, my company performed a written paint and body inspection prior to bidding, making note of any defects discovered along with photographs of any flaws. I examined the car while it was on the block, noting it was still in the same condition, and I ended up with the winning bid.

After the auction event was over, my transporter was delayed. It was picked up before the auction house's "must be removed by" date but several days after the auction concluded. Concerned that the car would be protected, I called the auction office to make sure that the car would be stored in an enclosed, secured building prior to pick up. They said it would. It was not.

Several days of cold desert nights and dust storms had their way with this concours award-winning magazine car. The car was so dirty when the shipper finally arrived to pick the vehicle up, that he had a hard time accurately performing a paint inspection. Nearly four weeks later, the car arrived at its destination, and we could accurately assess the Corvette's condition. It was evident that the car was exposed to the elements and was also the victim of some rough handling.

Most significant were stress cracks around the hood vents on either side of the power bulge, which was prominent on 1966 big-block Corvettes and is a common area of weakness on these cars. Stress cracks develop over time or can occur if the hood is repeatedly slammed by ham-fisted hands. There were also chips and scratches on other places on the car that were not listed in my initial paint and body inspection.

Immediately upon discovering that the car was not secured as promised and was no longer in the condition it was when I purchased it, I called the auction company with my grievance. It, of course, refused to take responsibility and denied that any of this damage was new or occurred when the car was under its care.

I offered my photos and written, signed, and witness-signed paint and body report from the event along with

acing page: Here it is right before it rolled off to wait in he staging lanes. It was gleaming so bright under those ights that it was almost painful to the eyes. Fortunately, he damage has been repaired to an undetectable standard, not that the auction company was any help. The uyer I represented used to buy two or three cars a year rom this auction house. Not anymore.

nother that was performed on the day the car arrived, long with transport bills of lading. The auction house aid it would review all of this and compare it to the nulti-angle video taken of the car while it crossed the lock. It asked me to be patient because it was still resetting everything back in its offices while also preparing or the next auction event. So, I waited.

A week went by. I called back. I waited more. I called ack the following week and asked to see the video evidence the auction house offered. I received another stall vith reassurance that it would cover the actual expenses f reconditioning the paint damage should the video eview yield that the damage was not preexisting. inally, two full months after I first brought the issue to he auction house's attention with no resolution, I sent vritten notice requesting mediation as per the contract. hey replied, referring to their bidder's contract which ead:

"Buyer must request a Request for Mediation form . . and submit the completed form in accordance with he instructions contained therein to begin the mediaion process. The form must be submitted within 30 days rom the date of purchase of the vehicle or Buyer shall be leemed to have waived and forfeited the opportunity to equest mediation assistance . . ."

So, the auction house never intended to remedy the ituation or take responsibility for how the car was stored nd handled while it was in its hands. I haven't bought nother car through this company. It was just waiting out the timer on the contract. Let my bad experience be lesson to others. Notify the auction house of any problems the moment they are found and *do not* let them tretch out the timeline for remedy.

Because I had my written field inspection, which was conducted before I bid, and I collected the transporter's ill of lading, including the paint inspection before it left, was able to demonstrate discrepancies to my insurance company. The damage was covered as a comprehensive laim. I let their subrogation department deal with the uction company.

The Corvette is once again in show-winning condiion. If the discrepancy occurred between pickup and lrop off, I would have done the same with the transport

company: call my insurance agent and let them battle it out with the auction company instead of wasting my time and sanity being fed lip service and excuses.

"I only bid on two kinds of cars at auction: unrestored, original-paint survivors and cars I know the personal history of," Tim Wellborn said.

The Car Isn't the Only Thing You're Buying

The most important thing a buyer can own about a car is the supporting documentation, which proves that it is real and right. Too many auction buyers spend their time in front of the car or in the beer line and never think to visit the most important office at the auction: the property room.

In this room inside musty cardboard boxes and crinkled manila envelopes lives valuable information that tells how a car looked before it was restored, how it was restored, how it lived its life, and what factory documentation supports the car's pedigree. Visit this place before inspecting the car. It provides context for the inspector that will better inform the evaluation.

The property room should also be the last place visited before leaving after purchasing a car. If at all possible, settle up with the cashier on the car the same day of the buy and take home the original documentation for the car that day. Auction houses are great at cataloging and keeping track of the items they are selling, but even then, things get lost or reclaimed by the seller. Even if they do send the original papers after the fact, there is a risk they can be lost in the mail.

I sold a 1970 Oldsmobile 442 W30 for a client who purchased it at auction. The car had a build card, which he checked to make sure was intact and readable before bidding on the car. He bid on the car on a Saturday and wired the money on Monday, trusting that all the factory documents would be sent (the build card and title). However, it was not until he went to sell the car that he realized the card was missing. Suddenly, his documented W30 was worth 25-percent less. Once original documents are gone, they are gone.

These steps may sound repetitive and tedious in each instance, and you are correct—this is the business part of the hobby that makes the fun part possible. A solid and methodical standard operating procedure (SOP) for securing, verifying, and completing a purchase is essential for preserving the freedom of enjoying big toys like these. That SOP, adapted to each purchasing situation, will make the difference between cracking a smile or clenching teeth every time you walk through your garage.

7 TIMING THE MARKET

This subject warrants a book all its own. At the most basic level, the market runs on two metrics: scarcity and excitement. The more excited people are to buy, the more they will pay. The rarer the automobile is, the more they will pay. If it is both rare and very exciting, the faster it will sell and for big money.

Scarcity and Excitement (Dealer)

Dealerships manipulate these factors in two ways. First, by presenting the perception that what it has is the best of its kind out there, and second by claiming it's pre-eminently rare.

Overbilling builds excitement in a buyer

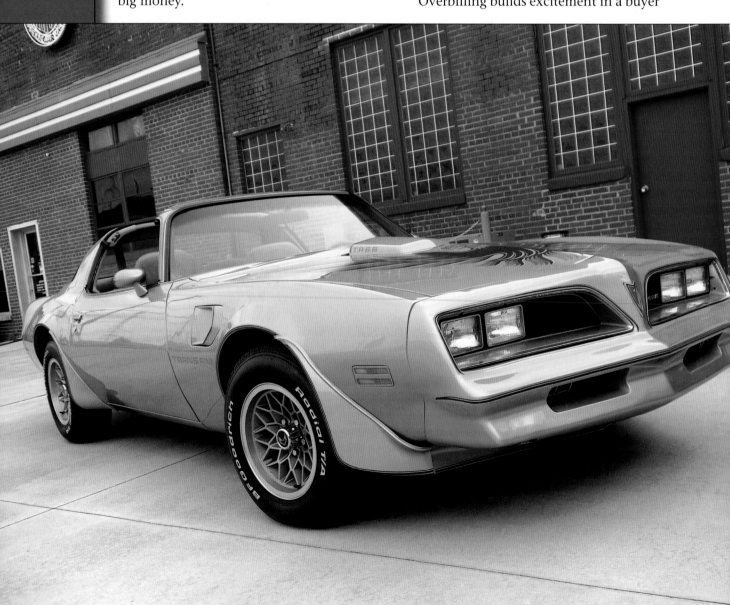

but inevitably leads to letdown and sometimes even turns to anger in a buyer once he or she discovers the true condition of the vehicle. Another way that excitement and scarcity are built at the same time is by highlighting the rarity of the vehicle.

> ## "Overbilling builds excitement in a buyer but inevitably leads to letdown and sometimes even turns to anger in a buyer once he or she discovers the true condition of the vehicle."

Most negotiations and purchase decisions turn on the shortcomings of a car. If you acquired the right car in the first place, then you are holding all the cards. You are no longer competing with a sea of other mediocre cars with excuses. This 15,000-original-mile, Unrestored as Factory Equipped 1978 Trans Am SE WS6 is in Excellent Plus condition. When the buyer is standing next to it in the showroom, yours is the only one and best available of its kind—the kind someone has to go home with.

The difference between genuine rarity (one of only a handful built in this drivetrain combination) and a manipulated rarity (one million were made, but this is the only one with red seat belts) is a matter of the degree and significance of the cited rarity.

In both cases, the end game is the same: "Come on down to the showroom and see it yourself." Proximity builds excitement. It is much more of a rush to see the dream car in person, being able to touch it, than it is merely to look at photos on a tiny handheld screen. Being in the showroom with the car also builds scarcity because, instead of being one of hundreds of cars on a car-buying app, this car is the only one in the room. It is the only one. The dynamic flips from seeking reasons to buy it to seeking reasons why *not* to go home with it.

Scarcity and Excitement (Auction)

The auction event manipulates these two factors as well but with greater effect. Overbilling is done with splashy catalogs, VIP invitations, and professional voice-overs complete with a video package on each car as it crosses the block.

Red carpets, flashing lights, cold beer, a roaring crowd, and the cameras—it is all built around excitement. The cars are almost coincidental. "We have excitement here, and we're selling some cars while we're at it!" This is reminiscent of the "Big Store" setups used by con artists and timeshare companies. Like the work of any good con artist, people say thank you for the experience before they realize they have been taken advantage of.

Manipulating scarcity picks up where dealer showrooms leave off: the car is real and in reach. Sure, it's not the only one in the room, but neither are you. Thousands of other people are wearing bidders' badges and ogling that car too. The kicker is that there is only 3 minutes or so to fight them all off to own it. *That* is scarcity manipulated to the max.

These two formulas have been around for hundreds of years. They may evolve to become more sophisticated and remain culturally relevant, but they are unlikely to go entirely extinct.

So, how can a private seller use these imputable motivators to always sell out of advantage without leaning on the crutches of old-school manipulation? It's simple. Present genuine rarity and true excitement.

Facing page: Pontiac's slogan for years was "We Build Excitement." By 1978, that meant a 220-hp engine and a giant bird decal stretched across the hood, affectionately referred to as a "screaming chicken" by some in the hobby. What made the Trans Am exciting was being featured in a hit movie, Smokey and the Bandit starring Burt Reynolds. Pontiac capitalized on the phenomenon by offering several iterations of the Special Edition (SE) package. That excitement remains a generation later.

The auction write-up for this car touted it as "One of the rarest versions of the second-generation Trans Am . . ." going on to declare the value inherent in "the Gold Edition's one-year-only exclusivity . . . This combination of rarity, factory equipment, low mileage, and documented provenance make this one of the most desirable Trans Ams in the model's history." These superlatives make it all sound like this is your only shot at ever owning one. While the Trans Am Gold Edition was only available in 1978, a production run of 7,768 does not qualify as rare.

Auctions rely on two human needs to succeed: a sense of group belonging or significance (everyone wears a number around their neck, even better if you are part of the inner circle by wearing a VIP badge) and uncertainty.

Uncertainty is the human need of variety. Uncertainty is the human need to know what something will sell for when the price isn't disclosed up front. The first is designed to make a buyer feel safe, the second is designed to intrigue with mystery and thrill with discovery when

the hammer drops. Significance and uncertainty/variety are powerful motivators that are core to our being. But there are four more.

Common Motivators

Understanding the intangible reasons that a person may buy a collectible car can be the key to choosing the most advantageous time to sell a car. I just covered how

This 2002 Ford Thunderbird roadster in Thunderbird Blue with full color accent package is perfectly paired with the original 1956 T-Bird sitting nearby. Ford jumped on the nostalgia bandwagon, building more than 68,000 roadsters from 2002 to 2005 after seeing Volkswagen reissue a contemporary take on its iconic Beetle and Chrysler cleaning up with the PT Cruiser. Nostalgia is a tremendous driver of demand for collector cars. The excitement of recapturing some of the magic of the original 1956–1957 made this a popular car when it was new nearly 20 years ago. Now, the 2002–2005 have developed a following of their own and prices are still below their cost when new.

The first-generation Nova is another example of a collector car that is currently affordable but poised to increase in the future with millennial collectors leading the way. If you are looking to sell your car that is uncommon and desirable but is not perfect, the best thing you can do is "hang a bell" on the shortcomings. The paint on this first-generation Nova Wagon is beyond worn out. The front fender shows some dings. Thirty years ago, you may have been tempted to run the car to Earl Shibe for a $49 paint job. Today, it pays to be candid. The paint is all but gone, but it reveals rock-solid sheet metal, which is a solid foundation for a future build. People pay up for good bones.

There is no mistaking a Fox Body Mustang LX as being rare. These cars remain popular today because they have been plentiful and affordable for years. They have their own subculture. One way to position yourself to sell out of advantage is to become a valued part of the classic car community. The comradery involved in buying an LX from another vintage Fox Body owner is just as important to a buyer as buying the car itself. People buy first from those who reflect their own identity and are committed to caring for same make or model.

few of these common human motivations can be manipulated by a marketplace environment to induce a high sell-through rate. Here, I outline which personal factors inform a purchase decision regardless of the environment in which the car is sold and how to appeal to them with integrity.

Certainty

People want to be certain of what they are buying, especially if they have also attached sentimental meaning to the item. That is why people hire a professional inspector, or at least bring a buddy to look at a car for them when they go to buy it. Facts over feelings. Data over drama. So, no matter the venue, represent your car candidly "warts and all."

When a buyer is certain a car is a good fit for his or her needs, it gives the buyer permission to get emotionally involved without the fear of being burned on the back end. Being up front with the flaws of a car or being clear about what it is *not* (they aren't all concours trailer queens) builds instant credibility, even if a person is otherwise a stranger.

Love and Connection

This is also about belonging but not in the temporary VIP-badge sense. This is about fraternity, being part of a community that shares your love for your favorite kind of automobile, dedicated to one another by shared enthusiasm. Being part of this kind of community (whether it be a social media forum or an international car club with a network of chapters across the world)

instantly builds trust between its members or thos seeking membership.

People are more likely to buy from and spend mor with people who share a common cause and kinship They could also be looking for a car to create more qual ity time with people they are already connected with such as friends and family. That is often more importan than how many NOS parts a car was restored with.

The significance emphasized should be that of th automobile. Genuine rarity is determined by outlinin; the reasons that a car is especially important and unique It is not about the red seat belts. It is the first of its kind the last of its kind, the most winning of its kind, the mos original of its kind, or the best of its kind. That is true sig nificance. When people buy a car like that, they do no need a VIP badge and 20 beer tickets to feel like they ar part of something important.

Contribution

A seller is looking for the next caretaker. No matte how the car was used or what the next owner plans fo it, it is almost always rooted in a need beyond their own Even if all they intend to do is buy a bunch of hot cars stick them in a building, and stare at them occasionally they are preserving a heritage and appreciation for these engineering works of art. They are treasure stored for th next generation to behold in awe. Restoring them mean giving their time and talent to give them a new life an meaning beyond their original purpose, which was to carry people around for three to five years and then head to the crusher.

ertain automakers, such as AMC, have had a small but loyal following despite the company being absorbed by hrysler decades ago. Because each owner sees himself or herself as a caretaker, not only of his or her own car but lso as an ambassador of the brand, significant models such as this AMX remain in the car collectors' consciousness ver the decades. As these cars grow in popularity beyond the generation that grew up with them, a new buyer isn't imply the next person to own the car but will be the next caretaker of the brand itself. The advantage here when elling is to find the person who is serious about taking on that role. They will be more selective in purchasing but also ay far more than the casual collector for the right example.

Others use their automobiles to raise money and wareness for charities that would otherwise gain little ttention. Sometimes, this sense of contribution is some- hing as simple as volunteering at a local car show. In the ase of many automobile brands that no longer exist, a uyer may not be simply seeking to fill a garage space but lso act as a caretaker or ambassador for the entire brand hat no longer has a company to preserve its heritage, elling its story to future automobile enthusiasts.

No matter what form it takes, people are fulfilled and appy because of the giving and service to others through heir enjoyment. Understand how a buyer is motived in his department and tell them how your car fits that bill.

rowth

Most people would read this as market growth: buy- ng low and selling high. Buying cars with meat left on the bone. This presupposes that the market is ever increas- ing, or in the case of contraction, winning off someone else's loss. Selling growth is more personal than that. It is helping other people find the cream as it rises to the top.

It could be selling them the nicest, most correct car they can find within their budget. It could also look like selling them the vintage race car that will help them bring their game to next level. It could be helping them find the car that will help them win their regional car show. It could be filling the next empty spot in their collection. It could be ending a lifelong search for the exact car they drove in high school. When selling a growth opportunity to a buyer, it isn't simply commodity futures, it is show- ing them the personal growth opportunity inherent in buying your car.

Presenting a car this way, congruent with a poten- tial buyer's sincere motivations behind buying it, creates

When selling a car that is not currently "hot" in the market but is certainly collectible, highlight how much work has gone into preserving and maintaining the vehicle so it is well positioned for future growth. The Prowler, built by both Chrysler and Plymouth, was a bold statement of design and engineering by a company demonstrating to the world that it was on strong footing and rooted in its past with a bold view of the future. They are rare by any modern manufacturing measure with 11,702 units from 1997 to 2002. One that has been impeccably kept with delivery miles on it and still bone-stock original down to the accessory belt and battery has a much higher potential upside to it than one that has been driven 15,000 miles a year for the past 20 years. People will pay more for good habits than they will a poorly kept car, no matter how rare.

demand independent from the ups and downs of the public sale market. You have heard them say, "The market may be soft, but good cars traded quietly are still bringing strong money." It isn't just that the cars are "good," it is that they clearly and assuredly meet these needs among people who trust each other.

Do the prep work to your car, or your entire collection, to make them the best they can be for how you most enjoy them. Then, communicate that to your network of trusted contacts. Even if you find yourself having to sell quickly, you will sell out of that advantage you took the time to build.

Trends

Money follows attention. Part of timing the market in the general sense is paying attention to what people are excited about. Ever since Ford announced it was res-

urrecting the Bronco nameplate, restorers, collectors, an custom builders have been falling all over themselves t grab any first-generation example they could find. As c this writing, buyers can expect to pay well into six figure for a custom-modified built Bronco. Originals in factory restored or original condition have also broken into si figures.

Toyota, likewise, rolled out a new Supra after th marque was mothballed for many years. The receptio by the enthusiast community was mixed—mostly due t focusing on the amount of BMW that was in the Toy ota. Nonetheless, previous generations began to receiv renewed interest and newfound respect among mor traditional American muscle and European performanc collectors. So, the skill comes with anticipating trend not merely following them. What is the next event tha will trigger a massive amount of public attention?

Here it is: the Ford Bronco. Until the last few years, most people didn't see old 4x4s as collector's items. The prospect of Ford resurrecting the once-iconic Bronco name-plate sparked new interest and new market oppor-tunities for craftsmen and enthusiasts. A custom vintage Bronco can be as expensive as a new Ferrari.

upra is another legendary nameplate. Toyota, pulling it out of the mothballs, certainly cast a new light of apprecia-on for the earlier generations. This one will be judged on how people remember those that came before it. This one, haring too many parts with its BMW platform sibling, may not reach the same legendary status. When that happens, rices for the originals often go even higher as people search for a classic instead of buying new.

8 PREPARING TO SELL

You have no doubt heard the following sayings:

"You make your money the day you buy a car and collect it when you sell it."

"A stitch in time saves nine."

"An ounce of prevention is worth a pound of cure."

Well, all of that is true when it comes to selling a collectible car.

A little bit of preparation work beginning on the first day of ownership saves a ton of frustration and hassle when it comes time to sell. To make selling a car easy and enjoyable when the time comes, get everything that belongs to the car from the previous owner before the deal even gets cold.

Get the Paperwork When Purchasing a Car

I cannot count how many top-shelf, investment-quality cars I have been asked to market for people, and when I ask the most common buyer question (if it has factory paperwork, a broadcast sheet, etc.) the answer is, "The guy I bought it from said he did, but he could not find it." Another answer might be, "He's still trying to find it . . . years gone by and nothing." The truth is that the seller never took full possession of what he or she purchased and now the car is worth as much as 25 percent less. Ouch.

I know that hurts. But this gets back to what I covered in the last chapter: certainty protects a buyer from being burned. Be certain of what is included in the purchase of a car and be certain to get it as a condition of the sale. Ask for photos or copies before signing a bill of sale. Make sure the documents and any spares are inventoried as part of the bill of sale. Lastly, make sure to have them in hand as a condition of the deal being complete. The paperwork should arrive with the car. If not, roll it back onto the truck and don't accept it until it does.

> "Be certain of what is included in the purchase of a car and be certain to get it as a condition of the sale."

A stitch in time: address it when the problem is small and the seller's mind is freshly focused on the sale and has incentive to find anything omitted. This saves months or years of chasing after someone who is no longer engaged, interested, or even remembers what happened to the missing documents. That is not fun. No paperwork as promised means no deal.

Being Organized Pays

It is surprising to me how may wealthy, successful, detail-oriented, Type A personalities I work with who run a tight ship in their business lives and are absolutely undisciplined when it comes to their car collecting hobby. As I've said before, the goal isn't to turn your car hobby into another businesses but to keep it from becoming another headache.

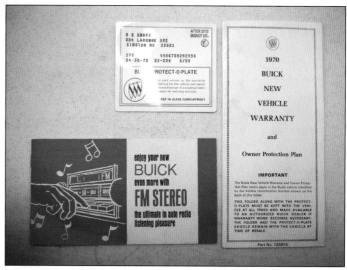

The documentation was as an important part of the purchase as was the 2 tons of steel, rubber, and glass in your garage. Protect them with the same veracity. Having documents like these safe, secure, and readily available protect the value of the car and create peace of mind.

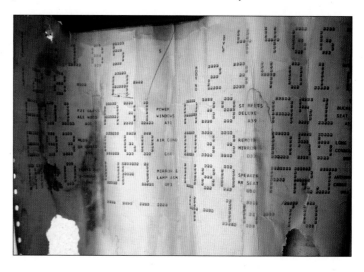

Keeping records on each car (or your only car) keeps the hobby fun and pays dividends when it comes time to sell. I suggest keeping original documents, previous owner records, and restoration/service receipts in a binder with plastic sleeves in a fireproof safe. In addition, I recommend scanning all the documentation and keeping it on an internet cloud file as well as a USB flash drive. Keep the flash drive separate from the paper binder, preferably in a safe deposit box. That way, if any of them are lost, then the others are preserved.

Also, keep a regular maintenance log for each car. Use a cell phone app or just a small steno pad and pen in the

Facing page: How much a seller earns on a sale isn't just an indicator of the market. It is a referendum on how well the person did when purchasing it and maintaining it during ownership.

Being organized is a matter of success in work. When it comes to hobbies, perhaps you want to relax and be less disciplined. That is a mistake. Being organized and disciplined in any collecting pastime wards off the specters of anxiety and disappointment. Keep the original paperwork in a binder with protective sleeves. Reproductions like this window sticker can be kept with the car to show friends and fellow enthusiasts.

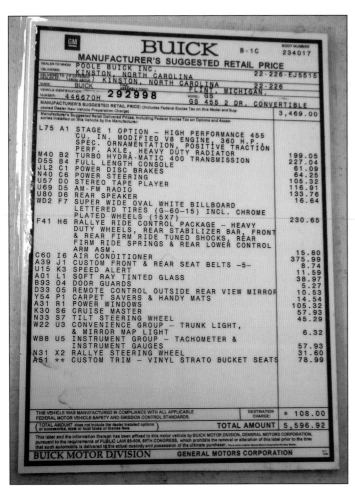

console. Either way, if a buyer asks when the tires were last replaced, the oil was changed, the fuel system was flushed, or the rear main seal was replaced, you have the answers.

Fewer people do this than you would think. Showing this level of attention to detail and ease of access inspires confidence in the next buyer. People understand that they are not just buying a car, they are inheriting the current owner's habits. Demonstrate good habits to build a reputation as the kind of collector people want to buy from. Eventually, your cars will be sought after.

Cashing in the Gold Mine: Building Pedigree Builds Value

People spend hours and hours (years even) looking for the right car and yet they spend very little time piecing together a car's past. It is harder today than it was years ago with changes in privacy laws governing dealership and auction transactions. Many times, buyers end up with a black box with no key. However, gathering a car's history can enhance a car's value.

A complete ownership history, the car's story, is as valuable as the quality, originality, or condition. Condition can be renewed, quality standards shift over time, and originality can be called into question without documentation to back it up. It pays dividends to fill in as many blanks as possible in a car's history.

Imagine spending money on a collector car and being told that it has documented factory paperwork only to discover that even the fender tag is missing. That is exactly what happened to this seller. Instead of doing what it took to recover the paperwork, out of frustration, he chose to fluff it up and dump it at the next auction. Predictably, he lost money.

his car is a 13,000-original-mile Hemi Superbird, Tor-Red with White interior. The documentation that comes with the ar is phenomenal. Each owner, including the first, was careful to keep it all intact and organized in one place. About 5 percent of the time, that doesn't happen and you have to hunt it down. The more history is established on a car, the ore valuable it becomes.

hese are two different tags for the same 1969 Road Runner. In 2009, the current owner of this car purchased it om someone who was on vacation but allowed the owner to see it. The current owner thoroughly examined the car nd determined it was a sound buy. What really could have aided the current owner was a Mopar fender tag expert xamining the car as well. The tag had been altered to "upgrade" the car with an air grabber and bucket seats. Other ptions that would never appear on a fender tag (G15, V3W) were either bogus codes or errantly applied. Fortu- ately for the current owner, he's a member of a 1969 Road Runner group where another member posted the original ender tag. Unreal luck. But the owner made his own luck by familiarizing himself with other Road Runner owners who elped him retrieve the original tag.

I had a client who was so excited by the prospect of Plymouth entering a winged car into NASCAR on its 50th anniversary piloted by Richard Petty that he purchased a 1970 Plymouth Superbird on impulse at auction. It wasn't what he told me he wanted (it was a column automatic instead of a console-shifted 4-speed), but it was real and right in front of him.

After the hammer dropped at nearly $121,000, he *then* asked the on-site Mopar guru to authenticate the vehicle. The good news was that it was a numbers-matching, original-drivetrain car in nicely restored condition. Some details, such as the position of the quarter panel "Plymouth" callouts, were in the wrong position. Bad news, the fender tag appeared to be missing from the inner apron, and the car did not appear to have any documentation. That isn't just bad, that's ugly.

Money Can't Buy History

Money can't buy history, but knowing the history of a car can certainly help a seller make money. No matter if a car was purchased out of impulse or a deliberate approach was taken to acquire a dream car, gather the car's history and discover its pedigree through research to enhance its value.

Yes, privacy laws and automotive sales industry regulations can be roadblocks, but buying and selling cars from collector to collector is still very much a social phenomenon. Most people are happy to share their experience with the car and any history they may have.

Know Your Numbers

Proving what the car is, rather than how it was represented, is vital in getting top dollar for the car when it's time to send it down the road. It isn't enough that the seller told you it was numbers matching. Look for yourself. Better yet, get an acknowledged expert to verify that it is.

If all the casting dates, assembly dates, and stamped codes on the drivetrain components are not already recorded somewhere in the paperwork, you have a weekend project ahead of you. Remember, if you can't prove it, you can't promote it.

Papers, Please

Factory documentation, while itself isn't guaranteed to be perfect, is the gold standard for verifying how a car is supposed to be equipped when it was showroom new. Cars older than 1998 largely must rely on paper docu-

At least the drivetrain numbers matched the dash VIN on the 440 car bought at auction, just like this Hemi Superbird. For most collectors, this is a minimum requirement to consider the car authentic absent of any factory-original paperwork.

mentation, but most every manufacturer has its production database available in some searchable form today. Just find the website relevant to the vehicle, enter the VIN, and get an equipment rundown on the car.

It would have been great to have that for LS6 Chevelles and 427 Corvettes back in the day. Still, there are other pieces of information that would be great to recover, including where it was sold when it was new, the number of miles that were put on it early in its life, and what modifications were done. This is where specialty vehicle registry information comes in handy.

Registry information is anecdotal and self-reported by previous owners. It is not as reliable as a factory database. Memories can be fuzzy about when they bought a car or from whom. People can be mistaken in reading an odometer or a casting code, or they can be flat out wrong about how the car is equipped, but it is still important for picking up some of those finer details.

Verify Before Selling

If the car didn't come with a third-party inspection report visually verifying and documenting how correct and original the car is, have it done before selling it. This kind of inspection can be used as a road map to make the car its "best self" and lend credence to any advertising claims. A third-party inspection is best used to corroborate what is self-evident or is already claimed in factory documentation.

The car appears to have the VIN stamped and original motor, and the casting code puts the block in the right date range when the car was produced according to the factory build sheet. The independent expert confirms that all these things line up, and further, the font

Here is the VIN pad on the engine for the same car. Between the two, having the original VIN-stamped engine is more important than the transmission for most collectors. On this car, the engine and transmission were stamped at the same time with the same tool. They should look very similar to one another. As I previously stated, for makers who incorporate the engine designation in the VIN, it is less crucial to authenticate the car, but for many concours collectors, it is no less desirable to have the original engine still in the car.

stamping, and surface of the pad are all consistent with known factory exemplars. That is what "numbers matching" is supposed to mean.

This type of inspection also shields a seller from a buyer coming back even long after the sale claiming the car was misrepresented. This is reporting what an expert's findings are about the car and not your own opinion.

Scrapbooking for Car People

The best time to catalog the myriad of minute details is during the restoration if the car is restored. All the components are out of the car and usually have been

cleaned and stripped of any paint, grease, or gunk, which makes stampings and cast codes hard to read and even harder to photograph. They need to be decoded anyway to ensure that everything going back on the car is date-code correct if not original to the car. Record all of it with photos, video, and handwritten decodes of all the major assemblies of the car.

It is one thing for an owner to know it's all original and correct. It is quite another to demonstrate that information to the next owner who wasn't around when you were knee deep in the project. Anyone who has been through a restoration knows how many thousands of dollars are spent getting the car back to its former glory. Memorialize the effort for posterity and put together a binder similar to the one that I described for the factory and historical papers—only this one chronicles the build from start to finish. Some folks balk at this idea. No one wants to see how the sausage is made—just the end product, right? Wrong.

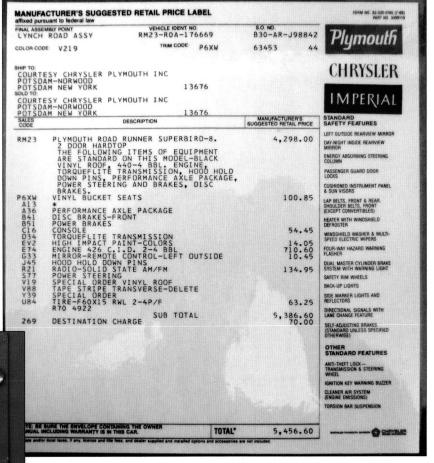

Here is the original fender tag for the Hemi Superbird. Having the original fender tag can tell, for the most part, how the car was originally equipped if one knows how to decode it on the fly. Having the original factory paperwork, including the broadcast sheet, the dealer invoice, or the original Monroney, will give enough information to have display pieces like this reproduction Monroney label accurately made. The buyer who bought the 440 'Bird at auction was able recover all the factory documentation such as this and more.

This 1967 Dodge Charger Hemi has the original engine. It also has OEM factory sheet metal, but the front passenger fender is from a junk yard donor. Look even closer and you can see this was also the case for the rear quarters. So, it's all OEM sheet metal, just not original to this car. The bottom photo is the car just a few years ago and about 20 years after the restoration. The bodywork has held up extremely well with no evidence of rust pushing up through the paint or bondo failure. Time is the best testament to quality bodywork.

A critical part of any no-excuses collector car earning top dollar is also removing any mystery about how the car was originally equipped or how it lived most of its life. Recovering the history and original documentation for the 440 'Bird was a tremendous victory, likely increasing the value of the car by at least 20 percent.

"It is one thing for an owner to know it's all original and correct. It is quite another to demonstrate that information to the next owner who wasn't around when you were knee deep in the project."

If the restoration process looks more like metal quilt making than it does car construction, then I sympathize. With that said, a new owner would rather understand what is under the paint instead of biting his or her nails wondering. Were the quarter panels replaced? Sure, they were. That fact is in the receipts. The restoration "baby book" shows how they were replaced using OEM panels

at factory seams to an undetectable standard. It's perfect; and there are no more chewed nails. Certainty breeds confidence.

Getting back to my client who impulse purchased the Superbird. While he made some critical errors, such as not having it inspected before bidding and not checking the property room to see what documentation was included in the sale, his researching skills saved him and turned what could have been a six-figure blunder into a bargain.

Researching the VIN, the internet turned up a previous auction where the car was advertised as having two owners from new, being an unrestored example in EV2 high-impact paint, and having two broadcast sheets and a fender tag. Well, several well-placed phone calls, texts, and emails later, not only did he recover the original fender tag and both build sheets but he also got in touch with the previous owner and original owner's family. In addition, the previous owner and original owner's family had additional historical documents and photos, including one photo of the car racing on the Baja Peninsula that showed the same "Plymouth" callouts in the wrong position on each quarter panel. Jackpot.

The seller who brought the car to auction for a quick flip invested thousands into refreshing and correcting the engine bay detail but missed the fact he had not recovered the documentation associated with the car. After auction fees as a buyer and subsequent seller, he was in the red. My client turned an ill-advised impulse purchase into an all-original body panel, 100-percent numbers-matching Superbird with full factory documentation and a pedigreed history.

Now, the Plymouth callouts weren't simply something wrong that was written off as a sloppy error committed by a flipper. they now had context, adding character to a unique car. With the historical photo, he could prove that they've been that way pretty much the car's entire life. Because of his research and recovery of this car's pedigree, that same car is now worth $160,000 or more today.

Preparation Summary

I know it all sounds like a lot of work. For some, this is their favorite part of the hobby. For others, the payoff of being organized and having a solid grasp of what a car is and is not comes when it is put on the market. Not only does it protect a seller from being in a weak negotiation position by discovering all the "unknown knowns" before a potential buyer does but it also shields the seller from any accusatory blowback after the sale.

A remorseful buyer seldom takes ownership of failing to do his or her homework or asking the right questions. They are more likely to blame the seller for withholding unfavorable information or failing to disclose problems with the car.

So, do the work. Find the history and preserve it. Research all the numbers and codes and record them. Chronicle the restoration. Document your enjoyment of the car for as long as you own it. Plug this information into the five keys of collectability to build the barstool for your car. This provides a clear snapshot of what makes your car an ideal fit for the next owner.

Confident buyers who are shopping for something as nuanced, emotionally charged, and complex as a collectible car can make a quicker decision and be willing to pay more for one with all that information. You are minimizing uncertainty, building value, and speaking directly to what the buyer values in this kind of purchase. A well-sorted, well-researched collector car is a tremendous story. Someone has been waiting to hear this story, which is perfect for them. Tell it.

Presentation

It isn't everything, it's the *only* thing. It does not matter how good a story a car has if a seller isn't skilled at telling it. A proper presentation helps the person on the hunt succinctly and immediately recognize that this is the one that he or she has been seeking. Selling a high-end collectible motor car without proper presentation is like if Pink Floyd wrote and rehearsed *The Dark Side of the Moon* yet never bothered to cut the album. If you weren't around for that one, songs from that record saw sustained radio play and remained on the charts for more than 17 years.

> "A proper presentation will help the person on the hunt succinctly and immediately recognize that this is the one that he or she has been seeking."

Correct What Is Possible

Most often, there is no business case for making a car perfect. I have written many times in this book that there is no such thing as a perfect car. There is, however, such a thing as making sure a buyer knows that your car is the perfect fit for him or her. The items to address when selling a car are those that will distract a buyer from seeing the car in its entirety.

Buyers want to see that the car is well cared for even though the seller is looking to move on. Whether going through the car yourself or looking over the results of a professional third-party inspection, remedy any item that would make the car unsafe to drive, is nonoperational, or is just plain missing. With a collector car, buyers pass on cars that come with headaches included. At best, they will use them as a bludgeon during negotiations and it will end up costing far more than it would if the detail were fixed up front.

Tires, the battery, fuel system, belts, hoses, and the like often need repair or replacement on a collector car that sees long periods of storage and is seldom driven. Make sure the tires have a recent manufacture date, have good tread, and the sidewalls are free of any cracks. If they are worn, rotting, or just plain old, replace them with the same kind as factory original. In the case of a custom car, replace the tires with those that have a

Now, it doesn't matter how well documented or rare a car is, if it isn't properly presented to the prospective purchaser, it won't get anywhere near top dollar.

peed rating compatible with the performance of the ehicle.

The same goes for belts and hoses; if they are hard, vorn, or cracked, replace them. Fresh rubber under the hood brightens up the entire engine bay. Check the undercarriage for any leaks. If you notice them, so will buyer, so address them. Sometimes an oil leak can be emedied with a simple oil change, retorquing of the gas-et bolts. Dried main seals can reswell from simply driv-ng the car or adding a conditioner without having to ull the engine and replace the main seals.

The fuel system is another area that is often neglected. f the car has been sitting for a while, run a fresh tank of gas with fuel-system cleaner through the car. If perfor-mance isn't smooth or improved, the gas tank may need to be cleaned or replaced, may need a new fuel filter, or even eed the fuel delivery system rebuilt or replaced. The best vay to prevent this type of pricey repairs is to not defer

maintenance in the first place. However, if a car doesn't run smooth and strong, there isn't much of a car to sell.

Lastly, check all the fluids and replace anything that is dirty or beyond its service interval. When it comes to the electrical system, test everything to make sure it is operational. Replace any bulbs that are burnt out as well as any blown fuses. The battery needs to be tested and most likely replaced. Other systems that are complex and given to failure from lack of use, such as air conditioning, need to be tested to make sure they work and recharged or repaired before offering the car for sale.

Assume the buyer knows nothing about mechanicals and would have to pay a shop a lot of money if he or she was to have these items fixed. Taking care of all these things up front and telling the buyer it is done creates a stronger negotiating position, builds value behind the asking price, and communicates to the buyer that you are the kind of person they want to buy from.

If purchasing a restored car, it's more than likely that the restorer kept receipts. If the car has changed hands several times, hopefully the paperwork has followed the car. Be sure to include all documentation when selling a car. (Photo Courtesy Michelle Kiffmeyer)

Clean and Detail

It is easy when a car has been let go in a seller's mind to also let how well it is cleaned and kept slide. This is a mistake. Perhaps the car has been sitting in the garage for a while and it is walked past daily but hasn't really been enjoyed, so, consequently, the seller decides to sell it. It is still a valuable collectible.

Dirt in the footboxes, cobwebs on the undercarriage, and flash rust or oxidation of any of the plated and bare metal surfaces can quickly accumulate and be easily overlooked. All these things, not to mention swirl marks in paint, crazing in stainless trim, or chalking out of black plastic components can cost hundreds, if not thousands, of dollars in the sale price or missed sales i he car is presented in this state of neglect.

Even if you feel like you are over it, make the car how-ready one last time. After all, collecting the money you earned when the car was bought is the most important show to prepare the car for. Without sliding into a partial restoration of refinishing or replacing parts, do your best to make the car stand tall with a deep clean and detail. If it makes fiscal sense, hire a professional detailer to go through the car inside and out and top to bottom so that no matter where the camera goes, it is capturing beauty and not an easily remedied eyesore.

If there are one or two blemishes or defects in the interior or paint and fixing them will dramatically enhance the condition of the entire car, repair or replace them. Use good judgment and pick a definite line not to cross. Whatever isn't fixed, be sure to call it out in the photos and description and build it into the asking price so that it is not used against you later when dickering over the sale price.

Photography and Video

The biggest part of telling the car's story is getting good photos and video of the car. Even if there is an impressive camera on your phone, it is best to employ the services of a professional photographer. Professional photographers are skilled at selecting the right location, ideal lighting, and the best angles to show off a collector car's beauty. If shooting the car yourself, stay away from photographing it on gravel or grass. Cows live in pastures; cars live on pavement. That is where they should be showcased.

At the very least, a car should be pictured in full sun or full shade, being careful to avoid harsh shadows. The car should be thoroughly covered with multiple angles, and details should be highlighted in the exterior, interior, engine bay, and chassis. Even more important than showing how beautiful the car is, candidly capture any detectible flaws or damage you have chosen not to remedy. If it isn't repaired, disclose it. Candor is as important to a prospective buyer as condition and quality.

The video should include a walk around the car, a demonstration that all the lights and safety accessories are operational, and a showcase of the exhaust note of the vehicle. The sound is what excites people more than even the look of a car. If possible, record the car during a cold start, a short ride along going through the gears, and turning the ignition off. These elements give a buyer the sense that he or she is there with the car, and that person is more likely to make a confident offer without having to see the car in person for themselves before committing to an offer.

Displaying Documentation

Have every piece of original factory paperwork, previous owner documents, project and maintenance receipts, judging sheets, inspection reports, historical photos, restoration pictures, and everything else organized in a binder that is easy to flip through. Also, have a copy of each document digitized. Taking pictures of these documents is okay, but scanning them into PDF documents is better. Show them to the prospective buyer once they are qualified as a good fit for the car and have determined that they can afford it.

When the documents are shown online, redact personal information and show only pertinent parts (not the whole document). This makes it more difficult for bad actors to steal information or use the car's pedigree to create a clone or make fake documents for themselves.

Using the Right Words

Writing an effective marketing description for a car should be treated the same as a personal resume. The description is the car's qualification to be the best fit for the next buyer. During an interview with a potential employer, the conversation is usually a matter of the interviewer scanning the resume and asking questions based on what was written. How the resume is written dictates the form and direction of the interview. The content and flow of the car's advertising copy does the same for the email, text, and phone conversations with potential buyers.

> "Writing an effective marketing description for a car should be treated the same as a personal resume."

The best way to cut down on tire kickers and time-wasting conversations with unqualified buyers is to open with what the car is *not*. If selling to a seasonal driver, begin the description with something to the effect of: "If you are looking for an uptight trailer queen that has never spun its wheels on pavement, this is the wrong car for you." Then, describe the ideal use for the car, namely how you enjoyed it.

Go around each section of the car, exterior, interior, engine bay, and chassis and call out any shortcomings no matter how seemingly insignificant. Most people try to conceal or minimize any flaws, hoping that an excited or naïve buyer will overlook them. This puts the seller on poor footing for negotiations and gives the appearance of

Here is the engine bay of the 1971 Plymouth 'Cuda 383. While this is no high-priced Hemi car, it is still detailed out, clean, and correct as if it were sitting new in the showroom.

being either dishonest or ignorant about the car.

"Hanging a bell" or highlighting these potential liabilities minimizes their impact on the final sales price and boosts buyer confidence in the integrity of the seller. Negotiating expert and author Chris Voss wrote that this paradox is called an accusation audit in his book *Never Split the Difference*.

Front loading a description or conversation about the car with the possible negatives inoculates later discussions from the problems these issues would create if they were disclosed or discovered later in the process. You may be surprised how many buyers reply, "That's no big deal." This is also why super model Cindy Crawford colors her mole brown instead of using concealer. Did you even notice? People are often looking for reasons to say yes to purchase a collector car. If the nitpick disclosed up front is the worst thing about the car then the buyer can breathe a sigh of relief about the rest of it.

Use the vehicle description to grab attention, disqualify the wrong audience, quickly summarize its key strengths for the right buyer, and direct him or her to the conclusion that this car, your car, is the best fit for the buyer.

THE PROBLEM OF PRICE

9

"It's only worth what someone else is willing to pay," is the oft-repeated throw-away phrase when describing the value of vintage vehicles. It is admission by those who utter it that they do not know what drives the value of unique collectibles.

Here is another oft-repeated phrase: "What is the least you'll take?"

I like to reply without hesitation, "Good question. What's the most you are willing to pay?" Somehow, that sounds crasser to the buyer than the original question. I do not

know why it would. After all, it is the same question.

The fact is, as with any negotiation, the buyer wants the seller to tip their hand and

Price guides are good tools for popular, high-volume collector cars where more than a few always seem to be for sale. But what about models like this 1968 Pontiac GTO Ram Air I convertible? Very few were ever made, and they rarely change hands in the public marketplace.

Contrary to how price guides compile information, pinning prices to certain transactions recorded while canvasing public sources, collectible cars, and collectible items in general vary widely based on the five keys we outlined earlier in this book: desirability, authenticity, originality, pedigree, and condition.

tell just how much money they are willing to give up before walking away. Notice that the entire exchange is about will and nothing about the intrinsic value of the item being discussed. Where does back and forth begin anyway? The worst possible predictor of value is the number plucked out of a price guide.

Price Guide Limitations

The idea of price guides driving the direction of the market for collectible automobiles is puzzling. They are predicated on the same model we are all familiar with: nearest neighbor valuation. Let's say a house in your neighborhood sells for $300,000. It has three bedrooms, 2.5 baths, a 2-car garage, and a full finished basement—and it's just like your house. A real estate agent will tell you that your house is now worth $300,000.

That may work for the real estate market, but it holds no currency when talking about specialty collectibles. The main value driver for housing prices is location. The top three factors are, in fact, location, location, and location. When the zip code changes, the price changes—sometimes drastically.

Automobiles of particular interest are not tract homes or even used cars. It does not matter what the

local market is for them. In most cases, they are sought after worldwide. The individual traits of each vehicle inform their value far beyond general condition grading. As I have touched on in previous chapters, this formula is overly simple. The fact is, most of the factors that inform a given make or model's value are often not even considered in most price guide models.

Look up a price on Hagerty, and it states the following phrase on the bottom of some of the listings: "Colors can make an astonishing difference in both value and salability." Color is certainly subjective, yet it has a profound impact on price. There are so many more factors intrinsic to the value of a collector car that are not even acknowledged or accounted for in their valuation algorithm.

> ## "Color is certainly subjective, yet it has a profound impact on price."

Yes, they have different levels of price (Concours, Excellent, Good, Fair, etc.), but these labels are not backed by measurable metrics. What other desirable options are on the car? How original is this car? What factors

elative rarity is an important aspect of desirability. The year 1968 may not be the most favored year for the GTO, and 7,684 were produced, so they aren't rare, but when you figure in the 400 Ram Air I engine and the convertible body-yle, that number drops drastically to 92. For the GTO collector, that becomes a "Gotta Have It," which is also hard to nd, fast. It also makes it very difficult to get a good market read with so few examples to track.

ccording to the Pontiac Historical Society (PHS), which administers Pontiac's factory production records, only five lack-on-black Ram Air GTO convertibles are known to have been produced. This is the 400 Ram Air engine, which stained Pontiac as a serious contender in the segment it created: the muscle car. Further evolution of the Ram Air rchitecture, culminating in the Ram Air IV 400, would also make Pontiac the most enduring nameplate of the era, roducing high-performance cars all the way to 1974, when most makers gave up in 1970-1971.

Desirability is further boosted by every collector's "Gotta Have It" factor: the manual transmission. This Ram Air GTO is factory equipped with a 4-speed close-ratio manual-shift transmission that is backed up by a 4.33 Positraction rear axle. This car was designed to spin up the RPM and put maximum torque to the tires fast.

documentation supports the authenticity of this vehicle? All of these items significantly influence price, and yet they are not even considered in price guide valuations.

Price guide data is compiled from public sources, such as auctions and dealers that report their sales data. The representations of these data points are not subject to any independent grading system inspection. Their condition and quality are self-reported by the auction consignor or dealership. Neither can be called expert or objective, and both tend to overreport the quality of their sold offering.

Most often, the average car found at auction or mass-market classic car dealer is of lower quality than the pedigreed concours collectible that changes hands privately. A price guide publisher may have spotters at events, but it does not have trained experts for every single car they cover.

So, a higher-than-average transaction price becomes a substitute for the definition of what number-one concours is in their book. In reality, that car may barely rate as a number two in judged competition. In addition, most of the volume exchanged at public auctions is from one dealer to another, no matter if they are splashy nationally televised affairs or perennial regional events.

Originality is also a huge market driver for the Pontiacs, which is one metric that price guides tend not to track or figure into the valuations. While Pontiac has a database to protect the authenticity of the marque, Ram Air blocks were susceptible to failure, and era-correct replacements are not plentiful. For a short production run engine like the Ram Air I, seeing the XS code on the stamp pad is a relieving reassurance that the right block and the correct transmission are in the car.

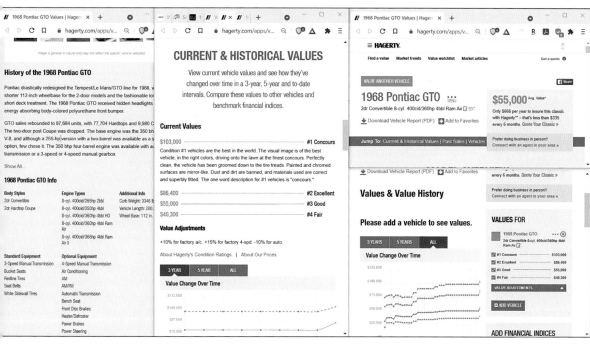

Ever look at a price guide, see a price, and say to yourself, "I would buy every example I can find for that money?" That is an indication that the guide is lagging behind a trend that it has not accurately measured or simply can't see. A price guide is only as good as its data source and sample size for every year, make, model, and trim level. If you are dialed into your niche, you have a more accurate understanding of market valuation than a large data aggregator.

Here is a 1968 Shelby GT500 KR convertible. About 512 were made, and there always seems to be a few changing hands every year. It should be a suitable candidate for relying on a price guide to get a handle on the best price to ask for the car, right? Not so fast. There are three keys that make this one hard to measure. Desirability, as this is a special-order yellow KR convertible. They only made a handful, and they are prized by competitive Shelby collectors. Originality, as this one is also a Division I Concours Gold Winner. Everything on the car is original restored or NOS. Pedigree, as the car has a known celebrity ownership history. All of these factors make the price guide valuation meaningless.

The more obvious factor that makes it hard to gauge price using an auction comparable is condition. Very few examples promoted as number-one cars ever meet the strict definition. This car has won Concours Gold in three national shows held by three different judging organizations and, at the time this photo was taken, remained in that condition. It is the very definition of a number-one car by any measure.

Very often what you are watching on TV is a wholesale transaction in public.

So, price guide figures are often lower than what the private market is transacting. They are good for seeing trends that have already happened or tracking similar lots at the same auction year after year to try to gauge value over time.

Guidelines at Best

Because price guides cover a broad scope of years, makes, and models, it is impossible to have consistently updated and accurate information on every single one. Most make and model pricing is extrapolated and not derived from recently recorded sales. So, price guides can provide an inaccurate read of the market or even the price trend if the model is rare or not often publicly traded. During the past 12 years, I have sold the same black 4-speed 1968 Pontiac GTO Ram Air convertible in a strong number-two condition grade to and for several different parties.

When the first transaction occurred, the best price

guide price that could be found was around $60,000. Those closest to the Pontiac segment of the hobby knew that only a handful of these cars were ever made and only a couple in black. Four times it has sold, each time for a little more than the last and closer to $100,000. Checking today, that same price guide shows a number-two condition grade car is only worth $78,000 and a number one is valued at $97,900.

The most desirable known example, only being excellent and not concours fresh, sold at or over that twice five years before. Price guides are more like guidelines and laws similar to the Code of the Pirate Brethren found in the movie *The Pirates of the Caribbean*. Sometimes, they simply do not apply. Use them to get into the ballpark but not as a substitute for appraisal or a collector's IQ.

When an Auction "Comparable" Just Doesn't Compare

The most easily accessible market information are auction results. On every source including television, online auction platforms, and social media, people are always discussing what cars at every level have sold for, from the swankiest live auction events to the bargains this week on eBay Motors. These results are well promoted by the auction outlets themselves: magazines and online forums are continuously hungry for new content.

What sold this month and at what price is an easy story to write. What it means for the hobby makes for good social media fodder, especially when it seems entire segments turn on a single sale. Even if a seller never intends to consign his or her car to a live auction or even list it for sale on the ever-growing number of online auction platforms, the influence on perceived market value is considerable.

It all makes for great entertainment, but how does it really inform the value of the car sitting in your garage? When trying to place an appropriate asking price on your

car, are you playing Apples to Apples or Cards Against Humanity?

An apples-to-apples comparison begins with understanding that what is seen on the phone or flatscreen may not actually be how the car sits in person. Potential bidders have the advantage of seeing the car in person and getting a professional opinion before deciding how much the car is worth to them in that moment.

Auction cars are not condition graded uniformly. A car claiming to be in number-one condition doesn't mean it meets a commonly accepted standard. It means that the seller thinks highly of his or her own car.

Likewise, if the auction buyer receives a report grading the car as a number two or a number three, he or she will only bid to the level a decent driver deserves. However, everyone staring at their screens sees that car

This is the engine bay of another 1968 Shelby GT500KR that was described with a string of superlatives in the auction catalog. None of them were close to accurate. The difference between this engine bay and the previous one is plain to see. Price guides rarely audit the condition grade that was claimed in an auction house catalog description. If you were told your number-one concours car was now only worth X, citing this as the example, you would be angry and rightfully so.

Here is another lower-volume car, inaccurately represented by price guides for a different reason than small sample size. This 1970 Plymouth Road Runner convertible is freshly restored, highly original with 100 percent of its original sheet metal and drivetrain and fully documented. Price guide estimates were low. After digging into the numbers, only three unique cars had sold at auction in the past five years and one had resold or not sold repeatedly, skewing the numbers. Dig into the data and find out if a bad car simply recirculating is causing an artificial depression in the market.

Here is the original bill of sale for the Road Runner. The total cash price included sales tax and the documentary fee. Only $5, wow. When looking at sales data to determine the right price to ask, make sure to compare the total cost involved, not just the auction hammer price.

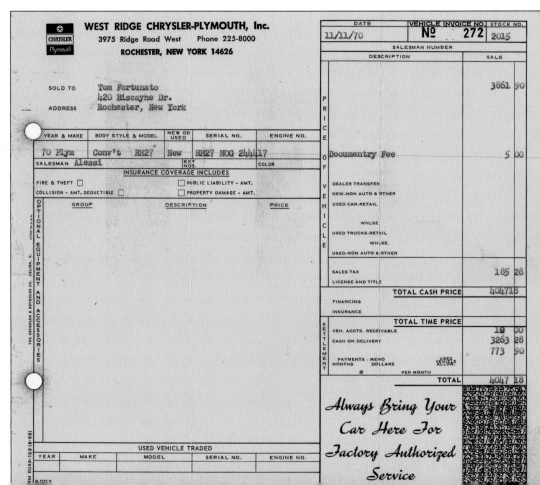

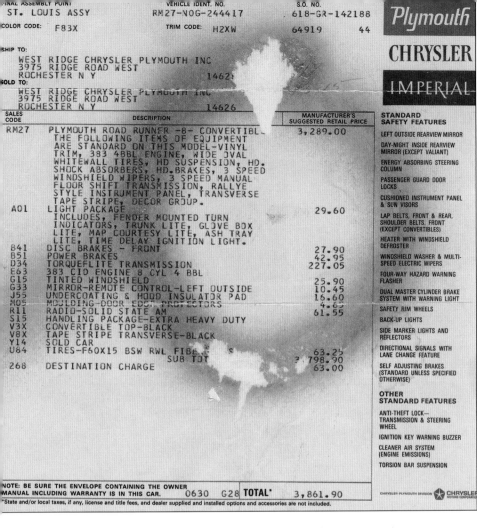

FINAL ASSEMBLY POINT · VEHICLE IDENT. NO. · S.O. NO.
ST. LOUIS ASSY · RM27-N0G-244417 · 618-GR-142188
COLOR CODE: F83X · TRIM CODE: H2XW · 64919 · 44

SHIP TO:
WEST RIDGE CHRYSLER PLYMOUTH INC
3975 RIDGE ROAD WEST
ROCHESTER N Y · 14626
SOLD TO:
WEST RIDGE CHRYSLER PLYMOUTH INC
3975 RIDGE ROAD WEST
ROCHESTER N Y · 14626

SALES CODE	DESCRIPTION	MANUFACTURER'S SUGGESTED RETAIL PRICE
RM27	PLYMOUTH ROAD RUNNER -8- CONVERTIBLE THE FOLLOWING ITEMS OF EQUIPMENT ARE STANDARD ON THIS MODEL-VINYL TRIM, 383 4BBL ENGINE, WIDE OVAL WHITEWALL TIRES, HD SUSPENSION, HD. SHOCK ABSORBERS, HD. BRAKES, 3 SPEED WINDSHIELD WIPERS, 3 SPEED MANUAL FLOOR SHIFT TRANSMISSION, RALLYE STYLE INSTRUMENT PANEL, TRANSVERSE TAPE STRIPE, DECOR GROUP.	3,289.00
A01	LIGHT PACKAGE INCLUDES, FENDER MOUNTED TURN INDICATORS, TRUNK LITE, GLOVE BOX LITE, MAP COURTESY LITE, ASH TRAY LITE, TIME DELAY IGNITION LIGHT.	29.60
B41	DISC BRAKES - FRONT	27.90
B51	POWER BRAKES	42.95
D34	TORQUEFLITE TRANSMISSION	227.05
E63	383 CID ENGINE 8 CYL 4 BBL	
G15	TINTED WINDSHIELD	25.90
G33	MIRROR-REMOTE CONTROL-LEFT OUTSIDE	10.45
J55	UNDERCOATING & HOOD INSULATOR PAD	16.60
M05	MOULDING-DOOR EDGE PROTECTORS	4.65
R11	RADIO-SOLID STATE AM	61.55
S15	HANDLING PACKAGE-EXTRA HEAVY DUTY	
V3X	CONVERTIBLE TOP-BLACK	
V8X	TAPE STRIPE TRANSVERSE-BLACK	
Y14	SOLD CAR	
U84	TIRES-F60X15 BSW RWL FIBE	63.25
	SUB TOT	3,798.90
268	DESTINATION CHARGE	63.00

NOTE: BE SURE THE ENVELOPE CONTAINING THE OWNER MANUAL INCLUDING WARRANTY IS IN THIS CAR. · 0630 · G28 · **TOTAL*** · 3,861.90
*State and/or local taxes, if any, license and title fees, and dealer supplied and installed options and accessories are not included.

Plymouth
CHRYSLER
IMPERIAL

STANDARD SAFETY FEATURES

LEFT OUTSIDE REARVIEW MIRROR
DAY-NIGHT INSIDE REARVIEW MIRROR (EXCEPT VALIANT)
ENERGY ABSORBING STEERING COLUMN
PASSENGER GUARD DOOR LOCKS
CUSHIONED INSTRUMENT PANEL & SUN VISORS
LAP BELTS, FRONT & REAR, SHOULDER BELTS, FRONT (EXCEPT CONVERTIBLES)
HEATER WITH WINDSHIELD DEFROSTER
WINDSHIELD WASHER & MULTI-SPEED ELECTRIC WIPERS
FOUR-WAY HAZARD WARNING FLASHER
DUAL MASTER CYLINDER BRAKE SYSTEM WITH WARNING LIGHT
SAFETY RIM WHEELS
BACK-UP LIGHTS
SIDE MARKER LIGHTS AND REFLECTORS
DIRECTIONAL SIGNALS WITH LANE CHANGE FEATURE
SELF ADJUSTING BRAKES (STANDARD UNLESS SPECIFIED OTHERWISE)

OTHER STANDARD FEATURES

ANTI-THEFT LOCK— TRANSMISSION & STEERING WHEEL
IGNITION KEY WARNING BUZZER
CLEANER AIR SYSTEM (ENGINE EMISSIONS)
TORSION BAR SUSPENSION

CHRYSLER-PLYMOUTH DIVISION · CHRYSLER MOTORS CORPORATION

Here is the original Monroney label for the same car. How many cars do you know of that still have their original window sticker 50 years later? This one document serves up certainty and significance at the same time, and people pay for both.

---

set the standard for a number-one price. The confirmation of this perception is complete when the price guide receives its spotter's report on the car billed in the catalog as a number one and publishes its new valuation, down 10 percent. Wow, says the internet, those cars sure took a hit this year!

So, before pricing a car based on the raw results of the last auction or the latest price guide update, do some investigating. If you couldn't be there to see it for yourself, find someone who was. How did that car really compare to the one you are selling? Adjust the number accordingly.

Also, pay attention to which cars are being used as comparable to yours. I recently helped a client sell a 1970 Plymouth Road Runner convertible. We were asking just under $80,000 because it was a fresh, driven show car quality restoration, was 100-percent numbers matching, had all original body panels, and had full documentation, including the original window sticker, original bill of sale, original broadcast sheet, and handwritten service history going back to practically new.

The public auction average for the car was about $55,000. Several people called to tell me I was out of my mind to be asking so much for this Dark Green car. One collector cited a red with white interior car that just

registered a "No Sale" at $45,000. His inference was that the market on 1970 Road Runner convertibles was so soft that even a desirable color combo was drawing little more than flies.

Well, it happens that his example car was one of many that floats from auction to auction without ever finding a buyer. In fact, five of the last eight reported sales of this year the make and model have been that very same car . . . through three different auction houses! It isn't that the market is weak. It is that buyers in the market for a car such as this are avoiding *that* car like it's COVID-19.

I cannot say what is wrong with the car. I have never seen it in person or inspected it, but the numbers say there's something very wrong. This happens more frequently than you might even guess.

"Issue Cars"

Auction cars with known issues perpetually don't sell or sell at a low price only to pop up again at the next event on the calendar. These auction zombies have an outsized influence on the potential sales price for others like it and a negative impact on cars that are excellent in all areas. Using zombies like this one is what traps you in the game of Cards Against Humanity I mentioned earlier.

Most of the money that goes into a restoration faces the ground. It is important to show everything when presenting a car for sale. Perfect or imperfect, candid disclosure supports the asking price.

The bottom of this overbilled auction car was a real letdown. Disappointment is a force multiplier. For every dollar it may cost to fix or disclose something, it will cost a hundred if it comes as a surprise to your buyer.

> "Auction cars with known issues perpetually don't sell or sell at a low price only to pop up again at the next event on the calendar."

When setting an asking price, dig in and make sure there isn't an auction zombie killing the market price for your car. By the way, my client's Dark Green Road Runner sold later that year for a healthy $76,250. While not perfect, it was the best one offered to the public in about a decade.

The Devil's in the Details

Here's another thing to keep in mind when combing through auction results and playing "What's My Car Worth?" Auction outlets do not uniformly report prices. Some report without buyer's premium and some with, and that can impact price trends by 8 to 10 percent depending on where a vehicle sold. Sometimes the app or auction database will note the figure as "hammer price" or "final settlement price."

Always use the final settlement price when calculating the value of a car. The reason is simple. When a bidder raises a hand, he or she has already accounted for the fact that the buyer's premium will be added to it. That is

the definition of how a car is worth what a buyer is willing to pay. Just because it is auction house profit, doesn't mean it should be left on the table. The seller has much more invested in his or her car than any auction company, dealership, or broker.

Sorting through all of this can be confusing. Be methodical and remember to account for all the factors that matter (desirability, authenticity, originality, pedigree, and condition) at the levels that pertain uniquely to your car. Then, you will arrive at a value rightly deserving of a collectible automobile and be able to back it up with solid information the buyer will understand and appreciate. If you are not informed and confident about the price, the car will end up selling short, like a tract home in a declining community or a worse by-the-pound commodity. People buy significance, and if a seller can demonstrate that with certainty, they will buy that as well.

Candor, Not Perfection, Brings the Biggest Dollars

When setting a price for a car, take into consideration the flaws inherent to that car. People don't purchase perfection; they buy trustworthiness, and they buy for their own reasons.

I don't know how many times I've caught myself gasbagging away about how white-glove wonderful a car is before the prospective buyer stops me and tells me, "It sounds too nice to even drive. I'd be nervous to even own it." Ope! I assumed what he wanted. Big mistake.

People buy for their own reasons, not to a standard

ere is an example of the typical local cruise-night Restomod. It was born a 1970 Malibu in the same exterior color
ut with a column-shift automatic, 350 small-block, and green interior. The work done is solid, but the car is far from
osmetically perfect.

perfection. Too often, sellers make the mistake of over-
lling a car and permanently ruin credibility in the pro-
ss. People pay more for what they are confident in, not
hat is misrepresented as "flawless."

Misrepresenting anything on the car, even if it is
nall, can cost a seller the biggest thing: trust and the
putation of the seller and the car. Describe the car can-
dly, shortcomings and all, to help a buyer find what is
e best fit for him or her, make quicker decisions, and
y more money.

The seller gets to decide up front, before even posting
car for sale, what things he or she is willing to repair
d which he or she is simply willing to disclose. Price
ose not being fixed into the offering price. A common
yer negotiation tactic is to anticipate that the seller
s, even in some small way, misrepresented the vehicle.
e buyer will take an undisclosed defect and amplify

Here is a com-
mon example
of wear and
tear. The origi-
nal seat backs
were dyed
and reused
instead of just
buying new
ones in black.
With more
than $80,000
invested in
the build, you
would think they would have sprung for fresh plastics.
Issues like this undermine the quality of work evident
everywhere else on the car.

Ticky-tack things such as scuffs on the armrest should be addressed before ever photographing the car. Missing details like this leaves the buyer with the impression that the car was not well cared for.

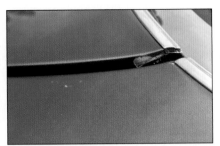

This chip inside the hood seam is a good example of an issue to document and disclose. Let the new owner decide how he or she is going to remedy it. If the buyer attempts to use it as a point for negotiation, simply state that the defect was considered when setting the asking price.

the cost to repair it or the value it has to themselves. A $100 repair can quickly become a $1,000 point of negotiation on price.

So, play offense. Tell them about the shortcomings the car has, perhaps even the estimated cost to address them, and share that those items have been factored into the asking price. The buyer is now all at once out of ammunition and disarmed. If the seller knows the car that well and is willing to be that candid, the buyer knows that he or she is less likely to end up with any nasty surprises. The buyer will also be more likely to judge the seller accurately as a straight shooter. The buyer can relax and negotiate from a more relaxed position. That is an advantage you want.

A Better Way to Determine the Asking Price and Get It

To arrive at the best asking price for a car, start with some baseline data. Instead of looking first at price guide data or even recent auction results, shop for that same car. If you were looking for that same car today, where would you go to find it? See what you will be competing against for the buyer's time, attention, and money.

Make note of how these cars are represented and what sellers are asking to get. If there are any currently up on online auction platforms, watch them. Pay attention to the questions people are asking and where prices seem to be averaging. Even better, network with fellow car enthusiasts. Find out who has sold privately in the past few months. Take notes on the particulars of these cars and how they compare with yours. As a last step, look up recent public auction results and find any cars that may conflict with or support your personal research.

These cars are less important to establishing an ask-

ing price but important when it comes to negotiating. A buyer will likely have done the same research but may have cherry-picked extremely low results to build his or her own price perception. Do not be taken off guard by an unknown and unfavorable comparison making a buyer sold on their idea of what your car is worth.

Price guide databases should be your last stop. Remember valuation indexes are not gospel; they are guidelines. See if the price ranges match your research. If your numbers are wildly out of range, find out if an auction zombie is depressing overall values. If your numbers seem low, find out if there have been any recent sales that really rung the bell at auction. This would be an outlier to the opposite extreme.

Dial these noisy numbers out of your data set and look for the signal. You want to be the best car offered of its like and kind but not at the absolute highest offering price.

Flip the Script

The best way to really figure the value of an investment collectible is to flip the script. Why did you buy this car in the first place? After all, you know what it took to find this car and get it to this level. You know what you were looking for, what options were the most desirable to you, and which were simply deal killers. People who will pay the most for your car are likely to use it the same way you have. That factor is called principle use.

> "People who will pay the most for your car are likely to use it the same way you have."

Using your own experience or the help of a local expert, choose the overall originality category that closest to how your car currently presents. Lastly, do the same for condition grading. These three factors together

The license plate reads MONEY, which is exactly what is at stake when properly preparing a car for sale. The goal is not perfection. There is no common definition for that idea in the car world. The goal is to make a car its best self when presenting in the marketplace. Put a spotlight on the strengths. Be candid with the shortcomings. Doing both will give the buyer confidence to pay the most he or she is willing to part with instead of the seller settling for the least he or she will accept.

ive the target buyer a clear and concise picture of whether the car is a good fit for him or her.

Next, use the barstool analogy outlined earlier in the book to come up with five bullet points summarizing each point of desirability, authenticity, pedigree, originality, and condition. The stronger each of these points are, the stronger the asking price is for the car.

The more clearly it is demonstrated that your car is a perfect fit for the next person, the more likely it is going to get your price. Most of the time, when collectible cars sell short of a well-researched target valuation, it because the buyer is dialing in on a discount for either uncertainty or carving out a budget to make the car a better fit for his or her own purposes.

Sometimes the uncertainties cannot be overcome, so price them in. When it comes to discounting a car because the buyer wants to take the car in a different direction, then perhaps your car simply is not a fit for them. That is their own indulgence, their own choice. Do not buy into the illusion that this is the only person with money. That is scarcity working against you. There is no need to subsidize the buyer's personalization of the car. You want someone who is excited about your car because it is the perfect fit. That is scarcity working for you.

10 SELECTING THE RIGHT VENUE FOR MAXIMUM RETURN

Now that the right offering price has been determined and it is clear how to tell the story of the car to attract the exact right buyer, the right place is needed to promote it. It is no different than fly fishing. You picked the right weight of line for the rod. You went out to survey the area around the river to see what insects the rainbow trout are hitting on this time of year to select the right fly. Now, the only question that remains is where you should enter the water.

Just Do It Yourself

The trendiest way people market a car themselves is to post it on a social media marketplace. They put up an eBay ad or even place a couple digital classifieds on Craigslist or Cars-On-Line with a few photos and a 45-word description. They cross their fingers and wait.

This approach is fine if selling a car that is, even for a collector car, common. There

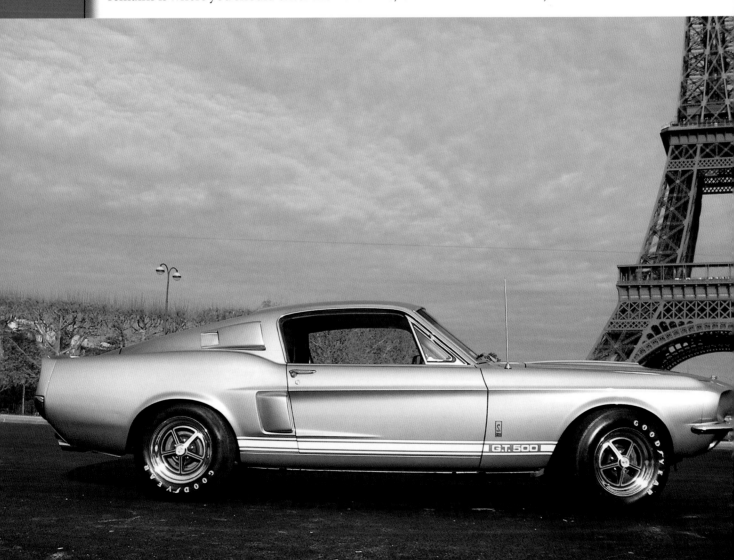

The last year of the manually shifted GT500s was 2014. To get a big supercharged V-8 from here on out, buyers have to settle for an automatic. This is a remarkably clean example with only 2,400 miles on it, which is a perfect addition for any Shelby collection.

Local and regional ads like those found on social media marketplaces are great for more common cars, but sellers usually get a combination of tire kickers, low-ballers, and outright hecklers when attempting to get collector-quality money for a low-mile car like this one.

Facing page: This 1967 Shelby GT500 was photographed in the bus turnaround in front of the Eifel Tower in Paris, France, back in 2010. Advertising this collection locally just wasn't working, so the owner flew me overseas to catalog and market it properly. Ripping around Paris in vintage Shelby Mustangs was a blast!

always seems to be one for sale and people are habitually looking for one, whether they are in the market or not. These are the Mustangs, Camaros, and Corvettes of the world that are usually found for sale among mass market transportation pods. They have an enthusiast following but are not limited-run special editions.

This is bobber fishing for bluegill, not standing in a cold stream trolling for brook trout. It makes sense if the car is high volume and high demand that has been driven about 1,000 miles a year. It's not quite a driver but not a garage queen either. These fall into the median price range for a given make or model.

Extraordinarily low-mile examples that are still in the wrapper and priced accordingly draw low-balling tire kickers and trolls bashing that higher-than-average asking price before it produces any qualified prospects. It really is not about a certain price point being the best suited for direct selling. It is about the comfort level of the target market.

Advertising on your own is most successful when the buyer is spending play money: their disposable income. When the relative price point begins to rise and so does the level of their discretionary income that competes with other potential investments, DIY advertising becomes less viable. There is a lot of junk to wade through on social media marketplaces and general classifieds in hopes of finding a well-sorted, investment-quality classic. Those who are looking for a place to invest in something that equals part fun and part profit are not likely to waste too much time combing through Craigslist to find it.

Online Advertising

Social media and internet advertising provide great exposure to a wide audience, but it also exposes a seller to spammers and scammers. Do you really want to spend your time on Facebook Marketplace answering dozens of "Is this item available?" queries only to never hear from them a second time?

There is also an inherent risk to advertising a collectible car on a format that also links to the seller's personal profile. If they have that for sale, what else do they own? Even public posts and information can be enough to lead a determined bad actor to a seller's doorstep. That is not the kind of "great exposure" they were looking for.

Privacy

When advertising publicly, pick places where the seller's identity and direct contact information are hidden. The objective is to protect personal privacy while getting the vehicle exposure. Also keep certain information

about the car private, such as the full VIN and clearly legible copies of the car's factory paperwork. Demonstrate that you have them, but only make them available for viewing once you have qualified a potential buyer.

Take steps to prevent the ad from being copied and used to defraud someone else. When the ad asks for the vehicle's location, use the biggest city nearby and not a small suburb. This makes the car harder for thieves to track down in case they have an unscheduled "test drive" in mind.

I would also recommend watermarking all photos and using an email address dedicated only to selling online. These two simple things will deter scammers from stealing the ad and protect a seller's identity from being stolen by someone catfishing classified car ads in search of their next mark.

Consigning the Car, Not Control

Let's say you are looking for bigger fish than bluegill or even the brook trout in your local stream. You may want to head to wider waters, but you will need an outfitter and a guide. That is when a specialty consignment shop or professional broker comes to mind.

Some are focused on a particular make or model and have developed a deep list of contacts within that segment of the hobby. You are using the relationships they have developed over time. Even if you may not like dealing with them at times, you end up doing so simply because they have positioned themselves as the gatekeeper of their domain. For the worst of them it is about control not your satisfaction or relationship, or that of the buyer.

Others are experts at how to market different cars to different audiences and know the right approach to reach the right audience quickly and efficiently. These marketing mavens have developed a healthy network of relationships across a broad range of hobby segments, makes, and certain high-demand models. These are lower margin, high-satisfaction services with a large and loyal following.

The last category of consignment shop is someone with a storefront containing a mix of their own inventory and private party consignments. These tend to be high-margin, low-relationship shops that continuously troll for new customers as they churn through those that they have already dealt with and left unsatisfied. Their marketing may be more ubiquitous than what an individual seller could manage on their own. They may even seem omnipresent, but at the end of the day, their reach has the same sophistication as a well-worded ad on a website like Cars-On-Line, Hemmings, or eBay Motors.

A car like this can be sent to a consignment shop that has a built-in clientele for cars of this type. Make sure they have a specific targeted marketing plan and they are not just doing what you could do on your own. Cars like this can get market stale fast, especially if they have the highest asking price compared to everything else around it.

After going through all the time and trouble of buying the right car and taking care of it all these years, protect your-self with a reasonable reserve. If the service is an online auction format, make sure the reserve is actually what you are willing to take. One tactic of a third party to secure the consignment and ensure a high sell-through rate is to prescrib really low reserves, telling the seller it should go higher. If they won't meet your bottom line, then it means the venue isn't confident it can deliver the best buyer. Find a place that can.

Four Things to Watch

Regardless of which kind of consignment service is chosen, there are four things to watch.

First, do you have the last say in price? Any contract signed should read that the seller has final approval or right of refusal of any offers submitted to the consignment shop. A dealer may negotiate a net minimum conveyed to you and then try to get 30 percent more on top of that to put in its own pocket. You may not care how much money the dealer makes as long as you net your minimum, but a price set too high could make a car get stale in the market and end up selling for far less than if the price were set correctly from the beginning.

You also do not want the consignment shop to sell the car short because it needs a quick turn, leaving you with far less than you would otherwise earn. You need to be protected from either extreme. A quality consignment service will recommend a reasonable reserve in writing, which acts as a floor for negotiations while they go out and earn the most the market will pay for your car, not merely return the least you are willing to take.

Second, do you retain possession of the title? How about the car? It sounds convenient to park a car at a dealer's showroom, but that also gives up legal control of the vehicle and sometimes the title. Some places that take physical possession of the vehicle and title as a condition

It doesn't matter if the car is a daily driver worth $10,000 or this Nightmist Blue 1967 Shelby GT350 worth about the same as a suburban single-family home. When a seller gives up possession of the vehicle and the title to any consignment shop or auction house, he or she surrenders a tremendous amount of legal standing over his or her own property. There are better ways to consign a car for sale without resigning control.

Facing page: These first two engine bays are the result of being in the hands of house mechanics the owner was entrusting to keep these cars in show-worthy shape. It was painful to photograph them in this condition, knowing the impression these otherwise fundamentally strong cars would give. Above: This clean engine bay is that of a 2014 Shelby GT500 in private hands. It still looks new. It shows the care taken by the owner to keep the car in this condition, even years after it was first brought home.

of consignment put the seller in a legally weak position to influence the final sales price. Courts have consistently sided with the dealer or consignment shop under this scenario. The net effect is that the dealer has an interest-free loan to keep the car until it sells it for whatever number the dealer deems fit, cutting the seller a check for the difference no matter how small the number is.

Find out who is responsible when a vehicle is damaged or requires repair while on consignment. If the shop takes possession of the car, make sure it is insured and maintain your own insurance until the car is sold. That way, it is covered twice over. Some shops take the car and store it for free but also offer a service inspection that invariably says the car needs more work than origi-

nally anticipated. Be sure the shop is trustworthy and not known for these kinds of underhanded tactics.

While the car is stored and for sale, the shop should have a clear schedule outlined to make sure that the seals stay supple, the gas stays fresh, and the battery remains charged. If it does not offer one, ask. The last thing a seller wants is for a car to sit for months and months unsold only to be returned needing all new engine gaskets, a fuel system flush and carb rebuild, and a new battery.

Lastly, learn how easy is it to cancel the consignment agreement. I have heard too many horror stories of unsatisfied customers wishing to remove their car from listing after two years and no credible offers only to find that they would have to pay 24 months of storage fees or

This 1970 Dodge Challenger R/T was not always the king of the auction block. Imagine if you owned it before the Hemi craze took off. If you have noticed an emerging trend and the price increases for a type of car you own, placing it in a competitive environment such as a live auction may yield a larger return than a traditional sale.

Sometimes, the car is so big you need to go big to get the best dollar for it. If you have a world-beating car and you want to attract the biggest fish, headlining a nationally televised auction event may very well be the best way to attract them.

Here is the moment of truth. This 1969 Dodge Daytona Hemi 4-speed wasn't the only car this collector brought to the dance. If you are going to make a splash, it better be a big one. We brought more than a dozen cars to market in that one moment, most of which had not been offered to the public before. That is how to build anticipation and excitement.

The reserve is off! A packed house and all eyes are on the big screen. This Daytona set a record, hammering for $900,000, and that's before the buyer's premium. That number has yet to be surpassed.

strong-armed into keeping the car there until it sells—no matter how long it takes. A reasonable consignment engagement is about 90 days. Good service providers will have an "out clause" no longer than 30 days so they can wrap up their sales activities.

A good consignment service can be an invaluable partner in the hobby, keeping it fun for the seller by shielding him or her from the risks to privacy and time wasters, as discussed earlier. Sellers also leverage the consignment service's knowledge, expertise, and relation-ships to earn more for the car than the seller would get on his or her own. In other words, it is a partnership that should pay for itself over time.

Auction Houses: Using Their Strengths to the Seller's Advantage

Given the tone and content of much of this book, it may seem as though I am anti-auction. That is not true. I believe in using the right tool for the right job.

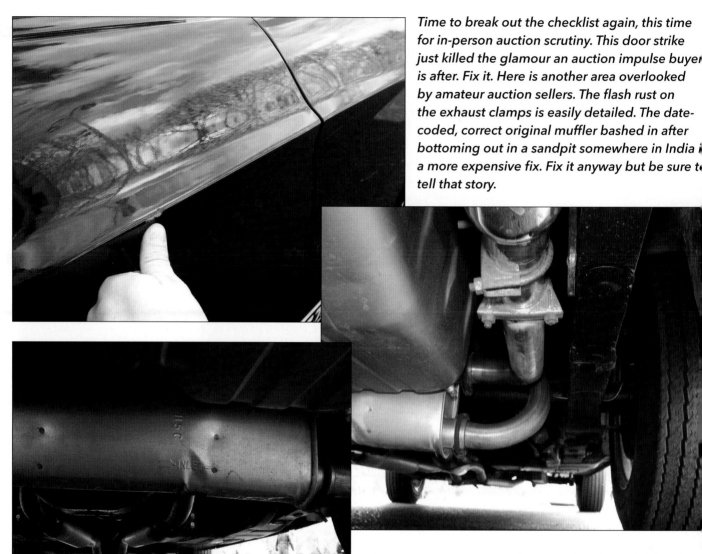

Time to break out the checklist again, this time for in-person auction scrutiny. This door strike just killed the glamour an auction impulse buyer is after. Fix it. Here is another area overlooked by amateur auction sellers. The flash rust on the exhaust clamps is easily detailed. The date-coded, correct original muffler bashed in after bottoming out in a sandpit somewhere in India is a more expensive fix. Fix it anyway but be sure to tell that story.

There are cases when it can absolutely be to the seller's advantage to bring an automobile through a classic car auction. If the car has been owned for a very long time so the "sunk" cost is low compared to the current market and it has not been offered for sale for a long time, the risk of losing money is low and interest in the car from auction regulars could be high. Noticing a car that buyers have not seen before plays into their natural desire for variety and competitive impulse to buy something others have not had the chance to buy.

Notice any emerging trends and price increases for the type of car you own and place it in a competitive environment like a live auction event or even a well-established online auction platform. This may yield outsized returns compared to a traditional sale. Although, timing such trends can be tricky business.

Another reason it may be a promising idea to con-sign cars to auction is if one make of model has been specialized in. Bringing the same types of cars of sound quality to the same auction event every time it is held fosters relationships and provides consistency in an environment that usually has very little.

This is a terrific way to build a personal brand or build a following for a repair or restoration business while standing out among the crowd of contenders. Keeping reserves reasonable so the sell-through rate is also consistent will have people seeking you out at auction.

In short, weaponize the auction fervor to create a gravity well around your car and what you are doing while limiting your exposure to risk. Make the house built for grabbing attention and building excitement focus most of its attention and excitement in promoting what you have.

Auction Contracts

Here are a few more things when choosing to bring cars to auction. Read the contract twice. Know your rights, responsibilities, and liabilities as an individual ealing with a large organization. The most important hing to find out is when you get your title back in the vent your car does not sell and if you are free to sell the ar on your own without penalty. Most auction houses all a 50-percent sell-through rate a success, so there is coin-toss chance you will be bringing your car home.

ime Slot, Time Slot, Time Slot

Yes, it is the real estate of auction events. For the car t top billing, getting the right time slot is not a problem. he entire event is organized around those cars. But even you do not have a headliner car, securing the right meslot is not just one of the things—it is the *only* thing. ars that sell early in the week or early in the day tend to ell for less money and often to wholesale buyers. If you annot be the headliner, then go for prime time. If you annot get a prime-time slot, do not go at all.

Do not expect to get a prime-time slot the first time ubmitting a car for an auction event. To secure a good lot, submit the car early and kindly decline anything ther than a Friday evening or Saturday afternoon time lot during the closing weekend. Usually, a quota-driven nside salesperson is tasked with the mission of filling housands of time slots for the next event.

Stick to your guns and make sure they know that if his one sells well, they are earning a new regular source f high-quality lots. That is the problem the auction ouse must solve. Once established as a regular customer, ou can position yourself to have your pick of time slots nd even negotiate a more favorable fee and commission chedule.

et a Reserve

The auction house wants a high sell-through rate, so will give an incentive to go "no reserve." For headliner ollections, some auction companies even give consign-rs guaranteed minimums. These are agreements to buy he whole collection on contract for a mutually agreed ninimum price. Anything over it is a split. If the car does ot meet the minimum, it can either go home with the eller or the house can pay them the agreed minimum no natter what it hammered.

This takes all the risk off the seller's shoulders and uts it squarely on the house. The bidders are the only nes unclear about who they are bidding against; each ther or the house that really owns the "No Reserve" car he moment the hammer drops and that undisclosed ninimum is not met.

For everyone else, the inducement to forego reserve rotection is much more modest. It is a discount on the ommission it will charge you or a better time slot. It

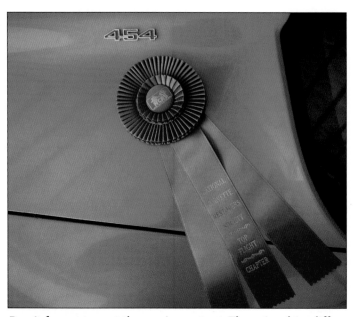

Don't forget to put the car in context. There is a big difference in perceived and real value between a car claimed to be original or concours quality and one that has won awards.

is reserve protection. Do not go into an auction unprotected. Figure the minimum needed to net after all expenses, set the reserve making sure all those expenses are covered, and stick to it.

Be Prepared

Prepare a checklist of everything that needs to be done to the car before it gets to auction. Inspect the car as if preparing for a judged show. It will be scrutinized as if it were. A small defect that was missed will undermine a buyer's interest in the rest of the car. Go over the paint and body, interior condition and function, engine bay detail, and mechanical inspection. From there, make a pick list and remedy each item. Once that is done, inspect it again.

Once the pick list is clean, include the final inspection report with the materials that will be displayed with the car. The average car purchased at auction requires 20 to 40 hours of skilled labor repair for it to live up to its own catalog description. Show buyers that they do not have a long repair waiting for them when they bring the car home.

Show and Tell

The most common mistakes sellers make when presenting their car boils down to one thing: taking all the mystery out of the car and putting it on a silver platter. Show potential buyers the quality and condition of the car with a professional, show-quality detail inside and

Presentation isn't everything; it's the only thing. This 1973 Corvette looks a whole lot more appealing inside this garage with a Daytona in the background than it does parked on the lawn by the car park. Between a polished presentation and a time-bound availability, cars that may be graded B for desirability sell more quickly.

out, top to bottom. Place mirrors anywhere they need to bend down to look for themselves.

In this day and age, show photos and video of just how clean the car is. In addition to displaying a binder with copies of all the original paperwork, show that clean mechanical inspection report. Show a video of the car running and driving as well. If the car is highly original and numbers matching, include a decode of all the numbers, photos of the stamp pads, and a third-party verification of their authenticity. Make it so easy for them

to love the car that they even forego having their own inspector look at it again.

In a target-rich environment, a seller wants his or her car to stand out in the potential bidder's mind long after the potential bidder walks away from it.

One more thing, always have someone who knows the car well enough to intelligently answer questions nearby so that any potential buyer can ask questions. Stay connected with whomever is with the car in case that person needs a lifeline or a potential bidder would

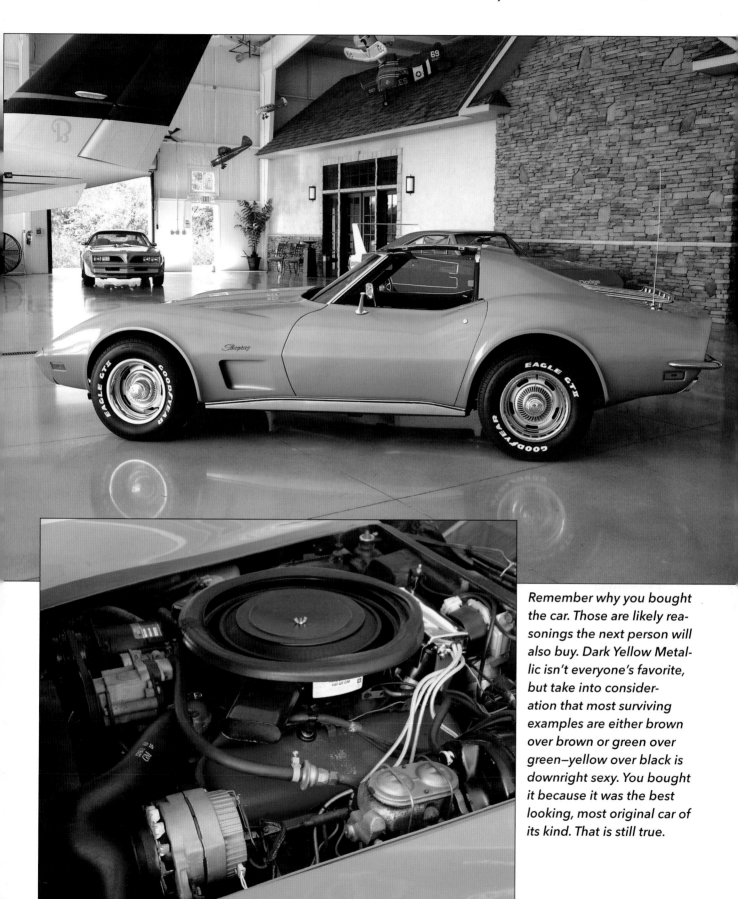

Remember why you bought the car. Those are likely reasonings the next person will also buy. Dark Yellow Metallic isn't everyone's favorite, but take into consideration that most surviving examples are either brown over brown or green over green—yellow over black is downright sexy. You bought it because it was the best looking, most original car of its kind. That is still true.

The interior of the 2014 doesn't need much of anything before being ready for market—perhaps a quick vacuum of the footboxes. The 1967, however, is in definite need of some TLC. After being driven road-rally style the length of India and then garaged in a country not very familiar with American muscle cars, it needs a spa day before it can be properly promoted. The interior needs a deep detail and wear items that have failed such as this door pull need to be replaced if the owner wants to recuperate the top dollar he paid when this car was a fresh restoration.

ke an introduction to the owner. People buy from peo-
le. The individualized touch in combination with the
xcitement-driven environment can mean the difference
etween a car doing okay on the block or smashing a
ecord.

he Seller's Judo Flip

One of the things auctions do well, whether they
re large in-person events or perpetual online affairs,
 shift the urgency from the seller to the buyer. It
 as simple as putting an egg timer on the sale and
viting everyone to watch it. The car suddenly

Suppose the strategy wasn't to get top dollar or simply minimize any further investment in the cars. Then, the next best thing is to package the entire group as is, where is, available only for a limited time. Take sealed, qualified offers and the highest one is awarded the group. It would have the same effect as bringing them to auction in this condition without the added expense of bringing them all to a venue and properly prepping each one.

It is easy to mistake personal affection for a car for its intrinsic value. When setting a price or considering an offer, remember this isn't about how much your love for the car is worth. This is now a business decision. Treat it like one.

becomes more desirable if it is only available for a brief time, building scarcity.

Take the auction environment seriously. If you are building a reputation as a purveyor of high-quality cars, then sitting around and sucking down free beers all weekend is a bad plan. Treat it as a business. Network, meet people, answer questions, collect contact information from potential buyers, and stay connected between auctions. Once you have built a big enough pipeline of people you know are interested and able to buy cars like those you have, you can do the same thing without even taking it out of the garage.

Instead of focusing on your want or need to sell the car, focus on why someone will want to buy. When someone inquires about the car, ask them how long they have been looking for a car before they ask how long yours has been for sale. Ask them how many cars they have looked at so far. Find out why each one fell short. You will soon discover that they are weary and frustrated with their search, desperate for it to end.

They will tell you what is important to them by telling you what they liked least about another car they passed on. They may even volunteer that they did find their ideal car but someone else scooped it up before they could put a deposit down. Their urgency is within each of those answers. Through skillful listening, you find out what you need to know to get them to commit to buying your car, now.

Promote Only When Prepared

Do not play footsie with the market by halfheartedly putting a car on the market with a few cell phone shots and scant details. The car may get some initial interest but blow a genuine opportunity because there is no photography, documentation, or answers people naturally ask for when they want to decide about a car.

People hate "hurry up and wait." So, do not promote a car until it is fully prepared, cataloged, and ready for presentation to a potential buyer, no matter how you bring it to market. Decisive people want all the information they need, right now, in the moment. Being organized enough to provide it right away, increases the chances of getting a positive answer exponentially.

Make Every Offering Limited

Nothing makes a collector car less desirable than being endlessly offered for sale, either for a prolonged period by the same person or over and over by a rapid succession of owners. Even if the car is fundamentally sound, a car that has gone stale in the marketplace begins to grow question marks. People begin to think there must be something wrong with it if it has not sold yet. Worse, some folks fill in those blanks for themselves and others.

Make certain that everyone who inquires about your car knows that it is available only for a limited time. It may not be a decision window as short as three minutes on the auction block or 5 to 10 days on an online auction, but make the offering time bound. Force them to decide or the opportunity will vanish. If the answer is no, this being the first time in 10 years the car has been made available for sale, you have no problem putting it away for another 10. There are no missed opportunities. Someone will always take them. It may as well be them.

Practical Pricing

Keep the price realistic and listen to all offers. Set the table by making sure the car is the nicest available in that price range and not the most expensive one out there. Use the higher-priced car, which is of lower quality, as a stalking horse for yours. When receiving an offer, no matter how high or low it is, ask the buyer to share how he or she arrived at that number.

Carmakers have gotten very good at injecting emotional attachment into their cars. Your name, Made especially for emblazoned on the window sticker, etc. Here they have even personalized the engine with the names of the assembly technicians. Remember that human need of love and connection? These tactics are designed to speak directly to it. It all feels good when you are going to buy, and it should. When you go to sell, leave it at the door.

When the buyer answers honestly, he or she will also share what the person values most about the car and what the person sees as a liability. Build on the value instead of reducing the price to ease the perceived risk. This approach will find the most a buyer will pay and not leverage the seller into revealing the least that he or she will take.

Once It Is for Sale, Consider It Dead to You

Detach emotionally from the car. Once it is offered for sale, in the seller's mind, it is already sold. This mindset will help you consider offers objectively, hear criticism of the car constructively, and help make it easier to say goodbye. Better yet, it will help you keep the memories of the car with you long after it is gone.

> "Detach emotionally from the car. Once it is offered for sale, in the seller's mind, it is already sold."

THE VERY NEXT THING A SELLER SHOULD DO

Now that one of your cars has successfully sold, part of that collection treasury is liquid again! Time for another one, don't you think?

Earlier, I touched on a few of the basic human needs. Enjoying a variety of beauty is one of them. When it is done right, collecting rare automobiles is one of the few ways to nurture this need without getting divorced or going broke.

Growth was another human need that I mentioned. Each collector is on a journey somewhere. Is it top grading a collection from a couple of driver-quality cars to a museum full of concours specimens? For some, it is making sure that the fastest car they have ever owned is the next one. For others, it is collecting the crayon box and assembling one of every color available in a given year.

Here is the result of one couple's quest in the collector car hobby. Not content with collecting and preserving what Plymouth actually produced for the car buying public, Gary and Pam Beineke took it to the next level and created real-life concept prototypes of vehicles Chrysler had planned, designed, and engineered but never produced. What is your plan?

It may be like my friend Steven who was taking the meaning of "restored to original condition" to its purest form. One of the last cars he had restored was a factory drag racing Cobra known as a Dragon Snake. He went so far as to find the artist who hand-lettered the car when it was new in the 1960s and bring him to the shop so that the numbers inside each roundel could be painted again. That is the pursuit of mastery. It also ended up being his contribution. His legacy was having the most correct and original restored and unrestored examples of vintage Mopars and Cobras for the rest of us to appreciate as the way they really were when they were new. That is a new benchmark for the next person to pursue and perhaps, one day, surpass.

Each time you buy a new car or sell the last one, the very next thing to do is take time to reflect on this crazy hobby of ours and ask the question, "Where am I growing next?" Chances are good that it is tied to one of those six basic human needs. Collecting cars is just a vehicle for fulfilling them. Being intentional about it will certainly help you get there faster.

Wherever you start or decide to take your car-collecting hobby next, the process and principles I outlined in this book will serve you well, just as it has some of the folks I presented as examples. Who knows, maybe your car or entire collection will be featured in the next one.

Facing page: Selling one or more cars isn't the end of something. It is an opening to the next possibility. So, take the time to reflect before jumping into the next car or on to the next pastime. You began with a vision, a collecting mission. What is the next step of growth?

Additional books that may interest you...

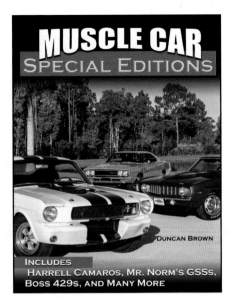

MUSCLE CAR SPECIAL EDITIONS
by Duncan Brown
Special-edition muscle cars are the highest valued and most collectible cars from American automotive manufacturers that were produced between 1961 and 1974. Muscle car historian Duncan Brown takes us through these special-edition muscle cars, their creators, and the behind-the-scenes forces that shaped these wild beasts into legends that left a lasting legacy. 8.5 x 11", 192 pgs, 390 photos, Hdbd. ISBN 9781613255797
Part # CT673

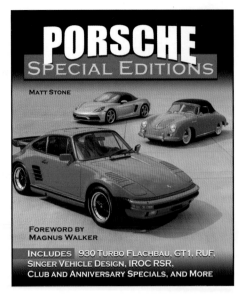

Porsche Special Editions
by Matt Stone
Porsche Special Editions contains a veritable smorgasbord of interesting, rare, and unique special Porsches from around the world. 8.5 x 11", 192 pgs, 457 photos, Hardback. ISBN 9781613257005 Part # CT684

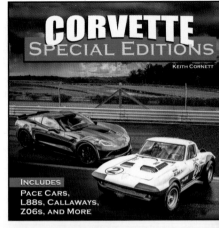

CORVETTE SPECIAL EDITIONS: Includes Pace Cars, L88s, Callaways, Lingenfelters, Z06s, and More
by Keith Cornett
Keith Cornett of CorvetteBlogger.com compiles a murderer's row of special-edition Corvettes in this first-ever compilation on the subject. This book is an encyclopedia of information, as you will learn about some of the rarest Corvettes on the planet. 10 x 10" 192 pgs, 481 photos, Hdbd. ISBN 9781613253939 Part # CT622

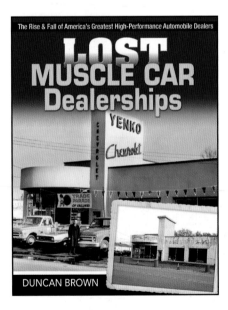

LOST MUSCLE CAR DEALERSHIPS
by Duncan Brown
Revisit the glorious 1960s and early 1970s, when cars from Reynolds Buick, Yeakel Chrysler-Plymouth, Mel Burns Ford, and others created the lasting muscle car legacy through innovative advertising and over-the-top performance. Detailed text and more than 250 historic photos and illustrations provide the history of those dealerships. 8.5 x 11", 192 pgs, 360 photos, Sftbd. ISBN 9781613254516 Part # CT644

Check out our website:

CarTechBooks.com

✓ **Find our newest books before anyone else**

✓ **Get weekly tech tips from our experts**

✓ **Featuring a new deal each week!**

Exclusive Promotions and Giveaways at www.CarTechBooks.com!

www.cartechbooks.com or 1-800-551-4754